C000212693

Redefining London
King's Cross
Bloomsbury
Covent Garden
Holborn
Soho
Fitzrovia

Edited by Andrew Mead

Essayist: Catherine Slessor
Design & Art Direction: Sarah Douglas & Lee Belcher
Photography: Dominik Gigler
Illustration: Peter James Field

Contributors: Rosemary Ashton, Simon Bradley, Dan Cruickshank, Gillian Darley,
Terry Farrell, Kathryn Firth, Malcolm Grant, Stephanie MacDonald, Roger Madelin,
Benedict O'Looney, Alan Rusbridger, Jonathan Sergison, Simon Silver, Mark Whitby

This book is published by New London Architecture (NLA) to coincide with the London Festival
of Architecture 2008. It is the first in a new series of NLA books, 'Redefining London'

NLA
Chairman: Peter Murray
Chief Executive: Jonathan Stock
Programme Director: Debbie Whitfield

New London Architecture, The Building Centre
26 Store Street, London WC1E 7BT

NLA is a Pipers project

First published 2008 © Pipers Projects Ltd

ISBN 978-0-9559569-0-4

A CIP Catalogue record for this book is available from The British Library

Printed by Creative Group London, Ltd

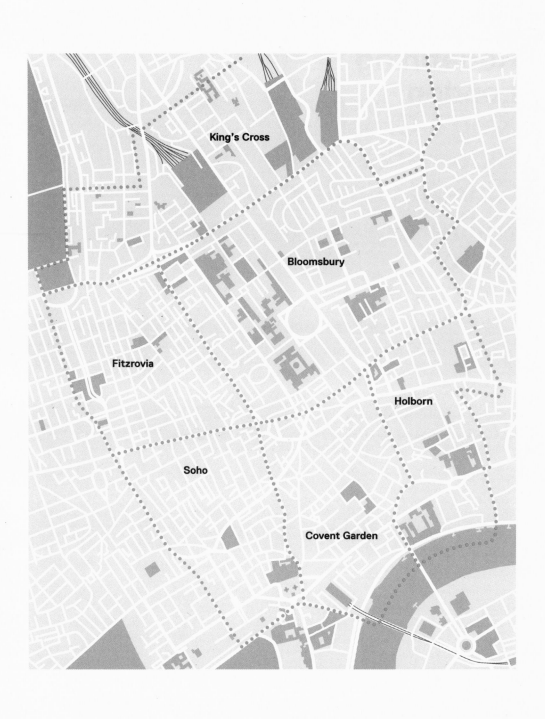

King's Cross

Bloomsbury

Fitzrovia

Holborn

Soho

Covent Garden

Contents

Foreword _____ 005
An introduction by *Malcolm Grant*, Provost
and President of University College London

A Pact With The Past _____ 007
A conflict between development and conservation
has shaped this part of London. *Andrew Mead* explores
its history and consequences

Building In Context _____ 043
Despite the emphasis on conservation since the 1970s,
there have been some notable new buildings and renovations.
Catherine Slessor highlights the best of them

Portfolio: A Sense Of Place _____ 073
Photographs by *Dominik Gigler* convey the architectural
richness of central London, with buildings that span the
last three centuries

Constructing The Future _____ 113
Masterplans that will guide future development
and some prestigious projects now under way

The NLA Sky Walk _____ 137
For the London Festival of Architecture 2008,
New London Architecture commissioned an installation
beside the British Museum by Carmody Groarke

Sightlines _____ 145
A collection of personal insights into these London districts –
their past, present and future

Maps _____ 161
A guide to the architectural highlights of King's Cross,
Bloomsbury, Covent Garden, Holborn, Soho and Fitzrovia

Foreword

by Malcolm Grant

I am delighted to introduce this book which is being published to celebrate the London Festival of Architecture 2008, but which will also be of value to anyone visiting this vibrant part of London in the future.

As President and Provost of University College London, I do, of course, have a particular interest in Bloomsbury. Alongside the notoriously unpleasant traffic throughways of Tottenham Court Road and Gower Street sit some of the capital's most attractive squares and institutions. The 18th and 19th century layouts of the parks, surrounded by solid and spacious houses, have been only partially preserved. It's now a hybrid streetscape – part residential and part-institutional.

The squares are bordered by Bloomsbury's intellectual giants. Among the early arrivals were the British Museum and University College London, the latter founded in 1826 as London's first (and England's third) university. With UCL came University College Hospital, now one of the world's leading clinical facilities. The 20th century brought Senate House and the cluster of colleges, institutes and schools around it. But the architectural design was at times depressingly poor. Utilitarian structures were squeezed into unsuitable slots, and no attention was paid either to their context or to the public realm more generally.

The 21st century is bringing new attitudes and welcome changes. Within Bloomsbury there are imaginative new buildings like the Wellcome Trust headquarters and the UCL School of Slavonic and East European Studies. Further afield, St Pancras Station has just been restored and the renovation of King's Cross Station is under way, while the former railway lands between the two stations are now the site of a major redevelopment. The proposed remodelling of Euston Station and arrival of Crossrail at Tottenham Court Road will complete a public transport infrastructure unrivalled in the UK.

In Covent Garden the new St Giles development by Renzo Piano offers a spectacular revamp of a sadly run-down area. A new approach to the public realm is arising from the stimulating work of Terry Farrell, in his masterplans for the Euston Road and for Bloomsbury itself. All of which makes the 2008 festival particularly timely.

This book is a snapshot of central London at a time of change. It gives us a glimpse of the future while acting as a guide to the many historical riches to be found here – the squares, streets and buildings. I'm sure you will enjoy it.

A Pact With The Past

By Andrew Mead

This part of London has seen a fierce struggle
between development and conservation
but do they need to be at odds in the future?

hen you want to capture the illusion of being in 18th-century London, take a walk round Bloomsbury's **Bedford Square**. You have to ignore the traffic crawling down one side of it but otherwise the square, conceived as an entity, looks much as it did when completed in 1786. The houses have mostly been converted into offices, so when night falls in summer they stay dark, but at dusk on a winter's afternoon the lights come on inside and reveal the plasterwork and painted ceilings, the decorative enrichment. This is quintessential Bloomsbury.

But if you leave Bedford Square at its north-east corner and walk into **Montague Place**, you find a very different picture. To the south is the long Neo-Classical front of the 1914 addition to the British Museum, John Burnet's King Edward VII Wing, while towering above you to the north is the austere Portland Stone mass of Charles Holden's 1930s Senate House and Library for the University of London. Apart from a glimpse of Gower Street, Bloomsbury's brick terraces have vanished.

Both the British Museum and the University of London have had a profound impact on the look of Bloomsbury today, but the plans they nurtured during the 20th century would have changed it even more. The struggle between development and conservation, especially as it came to a head in the early 1970s, is a key to understanding these Bloomsbury streets and squares – but also the whole large disparate area that this book covers.

In 1962 Philip Hardwick's noble 19th-century gateway to the railway system, the Euston Arch, was demolished – an event that fuelled the conservation movement, whose success came a decade later when it forced the GLC to drop plans for a wholesale transformation of **Covent Garden**. These events were crucial not just for the capital but the UK as a whole. The balance tipped emphatically towards conservation and created the culture in which architects practice now.

Covent Garden has a special significance in London's history because the square at its centre, built in 1629-37 for the 4th Earl of Bedford to designs by Inigo Jones, was the first to be created as the capital expanded beyond the City walls – and squares would become the drivers of London's future development. The one in Covent Garden, based on Italian examples and called the Piazza, was paved, but the next – laid out by the Earl of Southampton in 1661 and now known as **Bloomsbury Square** – was grassed, and this was the model for all that followed.

As fields were progressively annexed for building, these squares retained and fostered a green world at their heart. Each was embedded in a larger matrix of streets, shops, a market and other facilities – suburbs in miniature. They were usually developed by speculative builders who leased plots from the landowner. **Soho Square**, Golden Square, Fitzroy Square, and the squares that permeate Bloomsbury – these were the result.

It suggests a pragmatic attitude to urban development; a historically-rooted distaste for far-reaching plans. Perhaps that's a factor when we consider the turn towards conservation in the late 20th century. Only one attempt to design London on a truly grand scale has ever been realised, and it survives (albeit much altered) on the western edge of Fitzrovia and Soho. This is John Nash's scheme from the early 19th century for a 'triumphal way' linking Regent's Park to St James's Park via Portland Place, Regent's Street and Waterloo Place.

Bedford Square, 1775-86, is the most
intact and unified Georgian square in
London [Map p167 no.8]

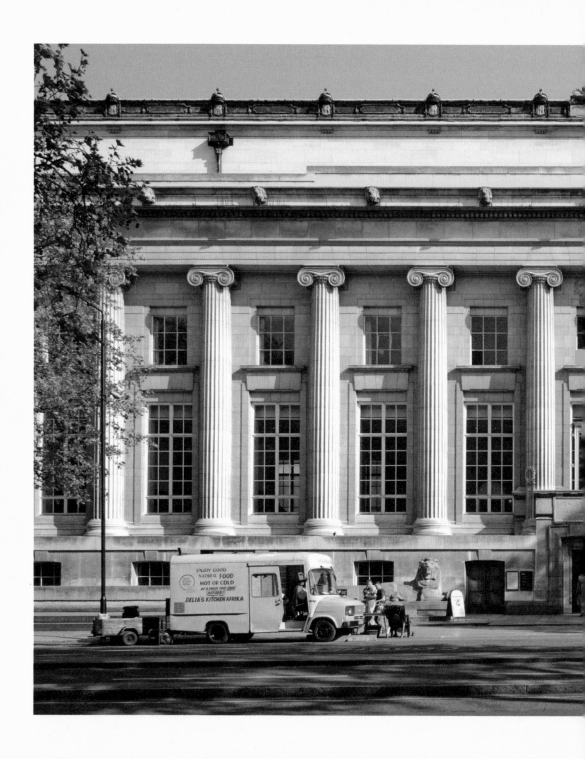

The British Museum's King Edward VII Wing,
1906-14, on Montague Place. Its architect
John Burnet envisaged three new wings but
only this one was built [Map p167 no.17]

'Holden proposed a long spinal building with towers at each end, a huge intrusive complex'

'Hundreds of old houses were demolished, businesses were moved, and the conflicts with residents were innumerable,' writes the historian Peter Whitfield in his study of London's growth as revealed in maps (*1*). Such 'conflicts with residents' would recur throughout Bloomsbury and Covent Garden, and in pockets of Fitzrovia and Soho, during the 20th century.

The **British Museum** made the first inroads. Housed initially in a mansion in Great Russell Street, the museum became much more monumental with Robert Smirke's building of 1823-52, its Greek Classicism giving it dignity and authority. But by the early 20th century the museum was short of space and John Burnet drew up plans for its expansion. It seems extraordinary now, but the north wing beside Montague Place was just one of three that Burnet envisaged – a similar eastern wing would have demolished part of Montague Street, a western one part of Bedford Square. The First World War and a shortage of funds put things on hold, but the museum still had hopes of completing the scheme until the late 1930s.

After much indecision about where to site its precinct, the **University of London** finally settled on Bloomsbury in 1927 and the next grand plans for the area emerged. In the drawings collection of the Royal Institute of British Architects there's an intriguing sketch by Edwin Lutyens of a design for the 10 acre site, with twin towers that recall his earlier unbuilt scheme for a university at Lucknow, India – like many architects, he was loath to lose what seemed to be a good idea.

But Lutyens was not among the four architects that the University formally invited to submit plans for the 10 acre site. The eventual winner in 1931 was Charles Holden, whose humane, politely modern stations for the London Underground still make commuting more tolerable than it might be. He proposed a long spinal building stretching all the way from Montague Place to Byng Place, with towers at each end and wings branching off regularly at right angles along its length – a huge intrusive complex.

'From an architectural point of view this type of plan offers very grand possibilities for an impressive composition of the masses into one great whole...The design for the buildings is mainly of our time, arising out of the natural expression of the plan,' said Holden. One objector was a Holborn Borough councillor and former university employee, T L Humberstone. 'The Press, jealous guardian of the amenities of London, has been silent on the proposal to destroy Torrington Square and thus deprive the city of one of its "lungs",' he wrote in his introduction to a symposium he arranged to seek lay and professional opinion on the plans. Humberstone thought the scheme was 'fantastically silly and megalomaniacal' and urged that 'the idea of a single great building should be abandoned' (*2*).

By the late 1930s it was clear that funds were insufficient to complete Holden's design (by then revised), so only the southern part of the precinct – **Senate House** and its tower – really reflects his vision for this expanse of Bloomsbury. During the Second World War it became the headquarters for

This map shows part of Bloomsbury
in 1824 with its orderly layout of streets
and squares extending northwards

Clockwise from top: Holden's original UoL scheme, 1931; the Institute of Education with the five wings Lasdun first envisaged; Goldfinger's proposed office block at the south of Bloomsbury Square, 1962

LONDON AS A UNIVERSITY CITY: A GREAT TEMPLE OF LEARNING TO ARISE IN BLOOMSBURY.

A MAGNIFICENT NEW HOME FOR THE UNIVERSITY OF LONDON: A PICTORIAL PANORAMA SHOWING THE PROJECTED BUILDINGS WHOSE FOUNDATION-STONE WILL PROBABLY BE LAID THIS SUMMER.

Woburn Square in the early 1950s before the church and terrace in the foreground were demolished to make way for Lasdun's Institute

the Ministry of Information – the likely model for the Ministry of Truth in George Orwell's *Nineteen Eighty-Four*.

'The Ministry of Truth was startlingly different from any other object in sight. It was an enormous pyramidal structure of glittering white concrete, soaring up, terrace after terrace, three hundred metres into the air....' Orwell has changed the building material from stone to concrete and exaggerated the height but the sense of something 'startlingly different' can still be felt.

In the post-war period both the University of London and the British Museum came up with radical new expansion schemes in Bloomsbury, but also on the scene was the developer Hammerson with architect Ernö Goldfinger – best known for his later Trellick Tower housing block in west London. In 1962 they proposed a mixed development of offices, shops and flats on a site immediately south of **Bloomsbury Square**, including a 350-foot high block on axis with Senate House – 'a magnificent, thunderous conception' according to one commentator (*3*).

Georgian and Victorian buildings would have been demolished, but at a public inquiry the scheme had some influential supporters – among them the architectural historian Nikolaus Pevsner and the editor of *The Architectural Review*, J M Richards. Eventually the government minister responsible, Keith Joseph, turned it down.

Meanwhile the **British Museum** was eyeing land to its south, between Great Russell Street and Bloomsbury Way, as a new site for its library – then still in the famous Round Reading Room. The 1964 plans by Colin St John Wilson and Royal Festival Hall architect Leslie Martin would have erased these nearby streets, creating an open space between the main portico of the museum and Hawksmoor's St George's Church, with a courtyard surrounded by housing on one side and the library on the other.

The government rejected the scheme in 1967 after protests at the destruction of Great Russell Street – by now conservationists were making headway – but in 1973 the museum presented another Colin St John Wilson proposal for much the same site. A recent monograph on Wilson suggests it shows 'a humanist, anti-monumental approach...it's a building which is part of the street scene' (*4*). Again the government dropped the scheme and the British Library was eventually built at St Pancras.

Denys Lasdun's **Institute of Education**, marching down Bedford Way, is hardly 'anti-monumental' but it's only a portion of what he first envisaged. In 1959 Leslie Martin had drawn up an outline development plan for the university's precinct, which Lasdun scaled back, but even in its incomplete state his Institute and nearby SOAS Library extension required the demolition of some 30 late-Georgian houses. Only one of the five wings which were to descend towards Woburn Square from the spine of the Institute was actually built, but Lewis Vulliamy's early 19th century Christ Church was demolished in expectation of the second.

While Lasdun's Institute was being planned and part-constructed, so, just a few blocks away, was the **Brunswick Centre** – usually referred to as one of London's few 'megastructures'. Its architect Patrick Hodgkinson prefers to think that it's in the tradition of such developments as the Adam Brothers' Adelphi (now largely demolished) by the Thames near Charing Cross. Two long stepped blocks of flats face each other across a concourse lined with shops and other facilities, but they would have been much longer, extending

Clockwise from top: the Euston Arch, demolished in 1962 despite loud opposition; Hodgkinson's Brunswick Centre was meant to extend further north, as this model shows; Colin St John Wilson and Leslie Martin's 1964 scheme for the British Library

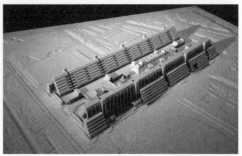

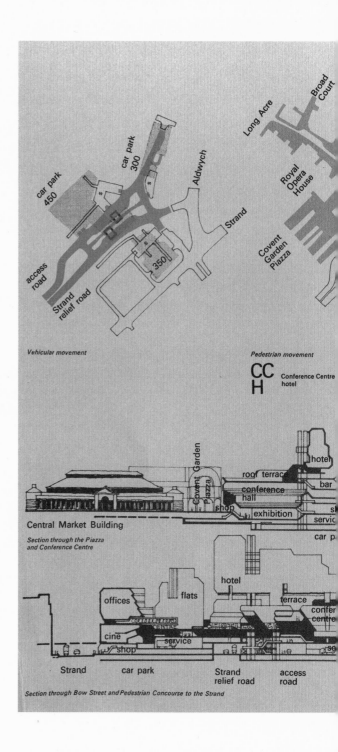

Vehicular movement

Pedestrian movement

CC   Conference Centre
H   hotel

Central Market Building

Section through the Piazza
and Conference Centre

Section through Bow Street and Pedestrian Concourse to the Strand

This spread from a 1971 GLC document 'Covent Garden:
The Next Step' shows some of the sweeping changes
that were proposed for the area. Their rejection marked
a turn to conservation in the UK as a whole

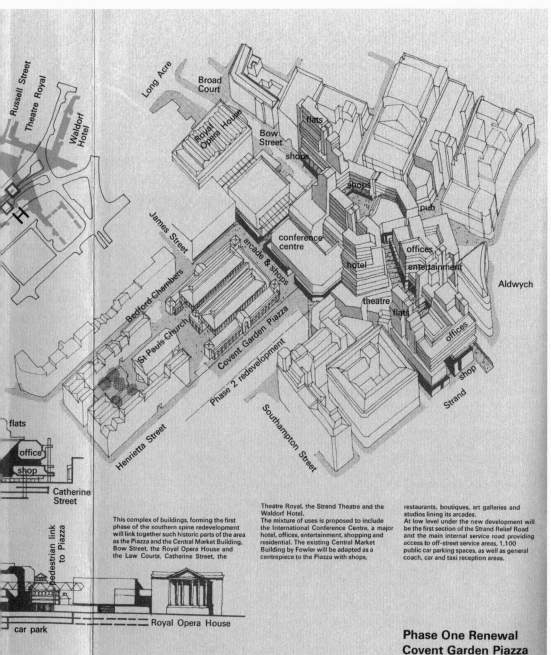

This complex of buildings, forming the first phase of the southern spine redevelopment will link together such historic parts of the area as the Piazza and the Central Market Building, Bow Street, the Royal Opera House and the Law Courts, Catherine Street, the Theatre Royal, the Strand Theatre and the Waldorf Hotel.

The mixture of uses is proposed to include the International Conference Centre, a major hotel, offices, entertainment, shopping and residential. The existing Central Market Building by Fowler will be adapted as a centrepiece to the Piazza with shops, restaurants, boutiques, art galleries and studios lining its arcades.

At low level under the new development will be the first section of the Strand Relief Road and the main internal service road providing access to off-street service areas, 1,100 public car parking spaces, as well as general coach, car and taxi reception areas.

**Phase One Renewal
Covent Garden Piazza
and the Southern Spine**

north to Tavistock Place, had Hodgkinson's plans (begun with Leslie Martin) been realised in full. Having taken over the project from the original private developer, the Borough of Camden halted building there late in 1972. 'It presented an opportunity to again bring together living, work and recreation to stimulate one another. It would have been a rich village,' wrote Hodgkinson in *The Architectural Review* (5).

So the post-war story in Bloomsbury up to the 1970s was one of ambitious projects that only partly came to fruition. Historic fabric was lost, disrupting the late-Georgian continuity of the area, but not on the scale that either institutions or private developers were happy to countenance. Outrage at the demolition of the **Euston Arch**, sanctioned by the government, had given a real impetus to the conservation movement and the tide was turning.

The Arch – actually a propylaeum – was completed in 1838; Hardwick's design derived from a ruin in Athens. 'That it would become the greatest monument to the passing Railway Age nobody could have known when it was built. But that is what it was,' wrote Pevsner. *The Architectural Review* referred to its destruction as 'The Euston Murder'; historian John Summerson called it 'vandalism of a disastrous order'. But significantly it wasn't just historians who protested – young architects such as Alison and Peter Smithson (designers of the Economist Building in St James's) joined in. 'If the arch had been a monument to Marlborough, they'd have found a reason for keeping it,' said Alison Smithson. 'It's a real catastrophe that travels round and round in one's bones.' (6)

Later in the 1960s the focus for conservationists was another station, **St Pancras**, where both George Gilbert Scott's flamboyant brick Midland Grand Hotel and the train shed with its sweeping iron arches were slated for demolition. This time the buildings stayed intact, thanks largely to strenuous campaigning by the Victorian Society and John Betjeman's persuasive prose.

But the defining moment in the struggle between development and conservation came at **Covent Garden**. The scheduled relocation of the fruit and vegetable market gave the planners some very big ideas. In collaboration with the boroughs of Westminster and Camden, the GLC devised a scheme whose effect stretched as far as Charing Cross Road, New Oxford Street, Kingsway and the Strand. It retained the market buildings and a mix of older properties (not just distinguished ones) in a 'line of character' running east-west through the centre of the area. Around this, however, the scene would be transformed, with new roads, separate decks for pedestrians, and a great deal of high-rise building – a radical change of character and scale.

'Specialist bookshops, bookbinders, mapmakers and dealers in stamps and curios are scattered throughout the area. There are timber yards and tinsmiths side by side with grocers and delicatessens...alms houses in secret gardens, black brick warehouses, shored-up castles of tenements...It is a finely balanced and working community,' said an article in *Architectural Design* in July 1971; but looking towards the imminent public inquiry it added: 'There is still time for a sensitive restructuring of the area, for nurturing rather than annihilating.'

Which is what eventually happened, as the protestors prevailed. Veterans of the earlier campaigns at Euston and St Pancras joined with community groups, shopkeepers, activists – a wide mix of people – in loud opposition. Although the government, when it gave its decision on the inquiry, didn't

Charles Holden's Senate House and
Library, 1932-7, towers over the southern
part of Bloomsbury [Map p167 no.33]

The university precinct, Torrington Square, is now
more coherent visually thanks to a landscape scheme
by Robert Myers Associates, 2006 [Map p167 no.55]

'In their scale, proportions and use of brick they play safe without resorting to pastiche'

rule out redevelopment in principle, it listed 245 buildings in Covent Garden at a stroke in 1973, and the plan was dead.

So what were the repercussions of this turn towards conservation, which the Prince of Wales would soon reinforce with some provocative remarks? If we return to **Montague Place** and walk towards its north-east corner, we can see one outcome – a building with a split personality by Shepheard Epstein Hunter. Stone-faced and with double-height oriel windows, **Stewart House** (1985) is vaguely modern where it faces Montague Place, but beyond a glazed link it sprouts a Grecian porch and turns into brick to line the west side of Russell Square in imitation Georgian. Could a willingness to compromise be more explicit?

It's a happier story a little further north in Torrington Square, where Nicholas Hare's **Brunei Gallery/SOAS Extension** and Stanton Williams' **Clore Management Centre** for Birkbeck College both enhance the university's precinct. In their scale, proportions and use of brick they play safe without resorting to pastiche. Clearly, though, there's no pleasing everyone: on Hare's building there's a plaque on which the university records its 'sincere apologies that the plans of this building were settled without due consultation with the Russell family and their trustees and hence without their approval of its design'. Fortunately there's a Civic Trust Award immediately beneath to put this admission in perspective.

Evolving in a staccato way, less comprehensively than either Holden or Lasdun had sought, the precinct is now quite satisfying architecturally; much helped by a recent landscape scheme by Robert Myers Associates which has introduced order into the previously disregarded centre of **Torrington Square**. Though the Bedford Way elevation of the Institute of Education is relentless, and the building's incompletion probably all for the good, its concrete towers form a striking backdrop – especially when dramatised by the sun. They supply a visual terminus on the east side of the precinct, just as the University Church of Christ the King and Senate House do on the north and south. The square has at last become a *place*, not a random set of buildings around a void.

With a new emphasis on conservation, properties that had become redundant couldn't just be swept away. Developers and architects had to find ways of adapting them to a different uses – as seen, for instance, in the reworking of old industrial premises in the **Regent Quarter** just east of King's Cross, a still distinct enclave close to the busy station.

By the 1990s, there was more confidence in juxtaposing old and new, not just discreetly tweaking a bit of historic fabric to insert a bar or a lift shaft – and more willingness on the part of clients and planning authorities to permit it. A prime example must be Norman Foster's glass-roofed **Great Court** at the British Museum; though some might think the museum's greater achievement was to leave those streets to its south untouched, where cafés, pubs and bookshops thrive to benefit all its visitors.

Stanton Williams' Clore Management
Centre, 1996-7, respects its late-Georgian
neighbours without resorting to pastiche
[Map p167 no.49]

Nicholas Hare's Brunei Gallery/SOAS Extension,
1995. Note the bold concrete rotunda as well
as the contextual brickwork [Map p167 no.48]

Denys Lasdun's Institute of Advanced
Legal Studies and Institute of Education,
1965-76, was only partly completed
[Map p167 no.39]

As for **Covent Garden,** Exhibit A in the conservation story – no-one can deny the public appeal of the revamped market at its centre, and if the character of the surrounding area had changed as drastically as the GLC envisaged, it would surely not have had the same allure. But sometimes the word 'heritage' seems synonymous with shopping – who knows how many clones of Covent Garden there are now?

To be fair, though, the Piazza does offer more than retail therapy. Overlooked by Inigo Jones' rebuilt but powerful **St Paul's Church,** it is a stage for outdoor performances and has a strong material presence – the stark granite columns around Charles Fowler's market, the stone slabs incised to help porters keep their footing, the cobbled floor.

A downside of the current stress on conservation is the tendency to think that if a building is old it should automatically be saved – one only has to remember some forlorn candidates for funds on the tv programme *Restoration* to see how entrenched that attitude is. With this in mind, it's instructive to look more closely at the historic fabric that falls within the compass of this book, so let's first turn back to **Bedford Square** where we began.

'It remains without any doubt the most handsome of London squares,' says the authoritative Buildings of England guidebook to the area (in the series that Pevsner initiated). Constructed soon after the 1774 Building Act which established four classes of houses, the dwellings are all 'First Rate' – the highest class – and today are Grade I-listed. Their future is secure. But writing in 1966, the influential, opinionated critic Ian Nairn thought the square was 'overpraised...Everything is hopelessly underpowered.' (7)

No previous London square was as uniform as this. **No 1,** designed by the architect Thomas Leverton, has an elaborate central doorway but otherwise the dwellings follow a standard pattern, with no special details apart from some delicate fanlights that are easily distinguished from later crude replacements. The square is generally well-maintained though there are signs of time and wear: some front-door stairs are chipped or colonised by lichens and the once yellowish brick now has a grey patina, so the cream stucco pedimented centres to each of the four sides stand out rather more strongly than they would have done at first.

Whereas some squares – Belgravia's Eaton Square, for instance – are simply too big to be experienced as an enclosure, that's not true here. It helps that the planting in the central oval is not so thick that views of the square's other faces are ever obscured, whichever side you choose to walk along.

For many years Bedford Square was a gated community – secure and socially exclusive. Its architecture suggests wealth but also reticence. Turn the corner into **Gower Street,** however, and do reticence and uniformity become something else?

'Almost wholly unadorned brick terraces, even, soothing, dignified, although certainly without much imagination,' says the Buildings of England. In his *Stones of Venice,* John Ruskin, passionate advocate for the Gothic, put it rather differently: 'Renaissance architecture is the school which has conducted men's inventive and constructive faculties from the Grand Canal to Gower Street; from the marble shaft, and the lancet arch, and the wreathed leafage, and the glowing and melting harmony of gold and azure, to the square cavity in the brick wall.' His contemporary George Gilbert Scott complained of the street's 'intolerable flatness'. Certainly Gower Street

The colonnade of Aberdeen granite that
surrounds Charles Fowler's Covent Garden
market house, 1828-30 [Map p169 no.2]

James Burton's Bedford Place, 1801-5:
a plain Georgian terrace in the manner
of Gower Street [Map p167 no.11]

is very different from, say, **Buckingham Street** near Charing Cross, with its
richly varied doorcases. But does it work as quiet background architecture,
formulaic but helping to make the city cohere?

That question recurs in Fitzrovia, whose architectural set-piece is the
scene that Henry Perowne, the neurosurgeon protagonist of Ian McEwan's
novel *Saturday*, gazes out on before dawn at the start of the book: 'the perfect
square laid out by Robert Adam enclosing a perfect circle of garden – an
18th century dream bathed and embraced by modernity, by street lights from
above, and from below by fibre-optic cables, and cool fresh water coursing
down pipes, and sewage born away in an instant of forgetting.' Only
half-completed to Adam's design, **Fitzroy Square** soon fell out of fashion
as Mayfair and Belgravia expanded, and its houses were mostly subdivided.
Today it still has a rather piecemeal appearance: not the perfection that
Perowne sees but a place where Adam's composition is undermined by
conflicting paint schemes and inconsistent maintenance.

That piecemeal look is a feature of Fitzrovia as a whole, but it proves that
modest Georgian buildings can readily accommodate a great range of uses.
Furniture-makers and other artisans had premises here in the past: now,
beside the bars and restaurants, are offices for media workers, engineers
and architects. This background architecture is flexible too.

In **Soho Square**, just south of the border with Fitzrovia, there's no
semblance of uniformity. Though there are fine Georgian terraces in Soho –
in Broadwick Street and Meard Street, for instance – the square has been
continually remade since the late 17th century. At its south-east corner is the
House of St Barnabas, once a refuge for homeless women but now an art
gallery, so you can step inside and see some of London's best 18th-century
plasterwork. Aston Webb's brick-and-terracotta French Protestant Church on
the north side is late-Victorian; so is St Patrick's on the east, with its tall red-
brick campanile. A 1920s office block has giant Doric columns. Styles and
materials change abruptly, the roofline soars and dips, it's a miscellany – but
it works. Soho Square is a convincing urban entity; no wonder the garden at
its centre is often thronged.

Not far from here is another garden, usually much less populated, because
for somewhere in the centre of London it's surprisingly hidden. The **Phoenix
Community Garden** is tucked between Charing Cross Road and Shaftesbury
Avenue, right beside the churchyard of Henry Flitcroft's 18th-century St
Giles-in-the-Fields. You don't have to be a botanist to see that the people
who look after it have coaxed a wide range of species, green and flowering,
into this modest L-shaped space, and have made every metre count in
creating tiny enclaves and pleasant spots to sit.

It has as its backdrop the spire of St Giles and Richard Seifert's **Centre
Point** office block – once routinely loathed, and a scandal for many years
when it remained unlet, but now a listed building. Tastes change – the
Buildings of England thinks it 'a classic expression of bright and brash
"pop architecture" of the 1960s' – and conservationists are quick off the
mark. But the view here will soon be different. A major development, Central
Saint Giles, is under way – not on the scale of plans for Regent's Place or
King's Cross but significant nonetheless, and with an international architect
on board, Renzo Piano. Despite the weight given to conservation in the last
30 years or so, the skyline is ever-changing. There is always something new.

Looking east across Soho Square to
the red brick campanile of St Patrick's
Church, 1891-3 [Map p173 no.22]

The Phoenix Community Garden with
Richard Seifert's Centre Point, 1959-66,
in the background [Map p169 no.36]

Denys Lasdun's Royal College of Physicians,
1961-4, whose Modernism is in harmony with its
Neo-Classical neighbours [Map p165 no.20]

A detail of Sir John Soane's Museum, 1792-1837, with its amber light and antique fragments. In the background is the Picture Room added by James Wild in 1889, where Soane's works by Canaletto now hang [Map p171 no.12]

So in thinking how the new might spring from the old without ignoring or simply replicating it, three sites in this book's area are worth a special look. The first is Denys Lasdun's **Royal College of Physicians** (1961-64) at the edge of Regent's Park – one of the best post-war buildings in London. Directly next to Nash's stuccoed Neo-Classicism, and with a Nash terrace opposite, it also shows that new can respond to old in an allusive, subtle way without losing its integrity. There are echoes of Le Corbusier (especially in the treatment of the topmost storey, which seems to float above the others) but in proportion and detail the college displays a kind of abstracted Classicism, and its white mosaic surface is as luminous as the neighbouring stucco. 'History is a useful servant but a hopeless master,' said Lasdun (8), though there's more give-and-take here than that statement implies.

The second is one of the Inns of Court that lend a collegiate character to an area stretching from the edge of Clerkenwell to the Thames. **Lincoln's Inn** is a harmonious whole but its buildings date from the 17th, 18th and 19th centuries and are varied in style. New Square's four-storey terraces are of brick; Robert Taylor's long Palladian block is of stone, and the sun prints shadows of the nearby plane trees on its white facade. Philip Hardwick's New Hall and Library are of brick again: they date from the 1840s but they are Neo-Tudor and their bulk brings a different scale to this carefully-knit complex. Like Soho Square, Lincoln's Inn has evolved over centuries in an accretive way, but by contrast its present unity isn't just a happy accident – it's calculated. Each addition to this ensemble of buildings and open spaces has been based on an appraisal of the overall site. Here new complements old to make a memorable place.

A few steps away across Lincoln's Inn Fields is our last destination, **Sir John Soane's Museum**. There's nowhere better in London than this intricate obsessive interior, with its antique fragments, mirrors and spatial ingenuity, to see an architect study, question and then transmute the past to make something of his own – something new.

Perhaps with precedents such as these in mind in future, conservation and development needn't always be at odds.

References and further reading
1. *Peter Whitfield, London: A Life in Maps. British Library, 2006*
2. *Thomas Lloyd Humberstone, New Buildings for the University of London: A Symposium. Dryden Press, 1933*
3. *James Dunnett, Ernö Goldfinger. Architectural Association, 1983*
4. *Roger Stonehouse, Colin St John Wilson: Buildings and Projects. Black Dog Publishing, 2007*
5. *The Architectural Review, October 1972*
6. *Alison and Peter Smithson, The Euston Arch. Thames & Hudson, 1968*
7. *Ian Nairn, Nairn's London. Penguin, 1966*
8. *William J R Curtis, Denys Lasdun: Architecture, City, Landscape. Phaidon, 1994*
See also three volumes in Nikolaus Pevsner's Buildings of England series (London 3: North West, London 4: North, London 6: Westminster), John Summerson's Georgian London, and Dan Cruickshank & Neil Burton's Life in the Georgian City

Andrew Mead is a freelance architectural journalist and editor

View north from Old Square in Lincoln's Inn
looking towards the rear of Robert Taylor's
Stone Buildings, 1774-80 [Map p171 no.1]

Building In Context

By Catherine Slessor

Despite the emphasis on conservation since the 1970s, these areas of London continue to evolve, as some notable new buildings reveal

hough this inner core of London might seem dominated by the weight of history, new architecture also flourishes. A consistent theme, however, is the need to respond to historical context, whether in the intelligent and undemonstrative urban repair underpinning the recasting of King's Cross, or through more elaborately conceived set-piece projects to revitalise great cultural institutions, such as the British Museum, the Royal Opera House and the National Gallery.

Individual new buildings are perhaps harder to pinpoint among the agreeable leafy squares, but University College London (UCL) has been an especially imaginative patron, not content to fall back on the safe-but-dull option of pastiche. Such expressions of vision by it and others add to the sum of an already rich architectural history.

Like thousands of hopeful northern provincials before and since, my first point of arrival in London was **King's Cross Station**. Back then, nearly 25 years ago, the area surrounding it was seedy and soul-sapping – its Georgian terraces rotting and unloved, its industry defunct, its railway lands a daunting *terra incognita*, and its roads clogged by fume-spewing traffic. It was a place to pass through, not linger in, and like all station hinterlands it attracted all the wrong sorts of people and activities. Nikolaus Pevsner describes it as a 'haven for noxious industries', albeit in the 1830s, but the epithet was still curiously apt over 150 years later.

There were the odd diamonds in the rough – the little backwater of **Keystone Crescent**, an exercise in bonsai Neo-Classicism, like a charming epaulette on an ogre's shoulder, while Houseman's radical bookshop kept spirits up during the Thatcher years and the Scala Cinema, with its triple bills of European art-house fare and American schlock, provided distraction and warmth on long winter evenings. But the spirit of the old King's Cross, of toothless, feckless despair, was perhaps best epitomised by the Flying Scotsman pub. Smack at the bottom end of Caledonian Road, this raddled old boozer boasted the last sawdust floor in London and ablutionary facilities so profoundly unsanitary that they were (allegedly) the inspiration for the infamous Worst Toilet in Scotland dream sequence in the film *Trainspotting*.

Today, while the Flying Scotsman still plies its trade with unreconstructed abandon and Houseman's celebrates a remarkable 40 years in agitprop, King's Cross is rapidly becoming unrecognisable. Like a long and dissolute acquaintance who suddenly decides to kick the toxins and get some cosmetic surgery, the effect is both disarming and heartening.

Current and future activity capitalises on a 'perfect storm' of development factors: an enviable proximity to central London, connectedness (two major railway termini), tabula rasa potential (vast railway lands stretching north to Camden), and the inherent robustness and adaptability of the area's industrial and historic fabric.

Now that the tide is turning, the **Regent Quarter**, a 5.8 acre site which adjoins the long, eastern flank of King's Cross station, is an encouraging sign of what might be achieved. As if in the hands of an especially determined nanny equipped with scrubbing brush and hot water, the decaying patchwork of Georgian and Victorian streets is being vigorously buffed up and restored to attract a new mix of uses. Shops, studios, offices, flats, even a hotel aim to reintroduce a sense of organic community, and though the architecture is undemonstrative, it is far from chocolate box, instead taking its cues from its

Tucked away close to King's Cross Station
is the well-preserved enclave of Keystone
Crescent, c.1845 [Map p165 no.5]

Part of the large area of former railway
land north of King's Cross Station that is
now being redeveloped [Map p165 no.29]

muscular surroundings. The scheme also involves running new pedestrian routes through hitherto inaccessible urban blocks, bringing life off the main streets into a network of humanly-scaled courtyards.

Further north, between York Way and the canal basin, is the nearly complete **Kings Place** development by Dixon Jones. Signposted by a fashionably serpentine glass facade on York Way, this seven-storey block might look like a speculative office but it has hidden depths, containing as it does a new 420-seat concert hall that will be a permanent home for the Orchestra of the Age of Enlightenment and the London Sinfonietta. There will also be a gallery to house the Borchard Collection of British Self-Portraits, a sculpture space, and a restaurant overlooking Battlebridge canal basin.

Brainchild of developer Peter Millican, this commendable cultural largesse is funded by 30,000 sq m of office space and is the first instance of local council policy that aims to support and encourage the arts through commercial buildings. In a serendipitous coup, Millican's first tenants will be the Guardian newspaper, which will occupy half the office space. Such a move is emblematic of a slow shift in the centre of gravity towards King's Cross as confidence grows in the area's potential, though it can sometimes be tough to be a trailblazer.

The arrival of Caruso St John's **Gagosian Gallery** to Britannia Street in 2004 marked a moment in what architect Eric Parry describes as 'the metamorphosis of this fascinating knuckle of London': the presence of an edgy contemporary art gallery is a reassuring indicator that an area is on the true path to regeneration. Caruso St John first worked on Gagosian's Heddon Street premises to create a series of intimate rooms for art; here they rehabilitate a former municipal garage to house a set of big, naturally-lit spaces capable of handling large-scale works by such artists as Cy Twombly and Richard Serra. Amid the mess and distraction of its surroundings the gallery appears as a typically self-contained, enigmatic presence, juxtaposing planes of dark brick with panels of milky translucent glass.

But there will be more to the King's Cross revival than the tactful re-use of existing structures. Behind King's Cross station lie great swathes of railway land, due to be the focus of a major development programme. Historically isolated from the surrounding residential neighbourhoods of Islington and Camden, this 67-acre site is a gaping hole in the fabric of north London, its industrial past still evocatively manifest in a decaying tableau of gas holders, warehouses and sheds.

Bisected by a canal and hemmed in by railway lines, **King's Cross** is a vast urban backwater whose time has finally come, after 20 years of political and architectural debate which spawned a series of unrealised plans for recasting the area. The most recent masterplan, devised by Demetri Porphyrios, Allies and Morrison and Townshend Landscape Architects, envisages a network of new public squares, tree-lined avenues, some 1800 new homes and 485,000 sq m of offices. Existing historic structures, notably Lewis Cubitt's Granary and the cluster of gasometers, are to be 'embedded' within the new matrix of development rather than conspicuously preserved.

Such ambitions have been given added impetus by the redevelopment of **St Pancras Station** to the west, as the site of the relocated Eurostar terminus. Once considered ripe for demolition, this infamous Victorian High Gothic time-warp is a remarkable story of survival against the odds. It was

In the Regent Quarter old industrial
buildings are being remodelled alongside
tactful new additions [Map p165 no.11]

'Over the last decade Bloomsbury has become more spruced up, like a cranky professor in a stiff new suit'

championed by genteel activists such as John Betjeman, whose statue now gazes up in wonder at the restored ridge and furrow glazing of William Barlow's soaring roof vault; the fickle wheel of public taste has come full circle, bringing the Gormenghast of the railways back into the fold. Now assured of the right kind of clientele, the former Midland Hotel (now **St Pancras Chambers**) is also due for refurbishment by the Manhattan Loft Corporation, so George Gilbert Scott's hectic fretwork of pinnacles, tracery, lancet windows and chimney pots will once again preside over its municipal fiefdom, like a medieval Flemish town hall transplanted to Euston Road.

In a generally well-orchestrated renovation, there are the odd duff notes. Required to accommodate extra-long Eurostar trains, the new, flat-roofed station canopy docks into Barlow's shed with singular gracelessness. And having appraised Paul Day's dismal 9m-high bronze of a couple (almost) canoodling, you might have need to adjourn to the much vaunted 'world's longest champagne bar' to numb your faculties.

To see how public sculpture should be done, stroll across to the Brobdignagian brick bulk of the **British Library**, west of St Pancras, where Eduardo Paolozzi's impressively mechanistic Newton dominates the library's generous entrance courtyard. Set back from the blare of Euston Road, Colin St John Wilson's magnum opus is a sensible Scandinavian riposte to Scott's Victoriana, its skinny, Aalto-esque clock tower duelling with its more blowsy counterpart. Two libraries, humanities to the west and science to the north, are accommodated in broad wings placed along the edges of the site, enclosing and defining the entrance courtyard. These are linked by a lofty public foyer into which cascades a grand staircase from the reading rooms above. Bureaucratic ineptitude and parsimony conspired to delay completion for 23 years, but it has proved a worthy repository of the nation's knowledge, superbly crafted and full of subtle rewards.

The British Library's move from the **British Museum** (the matron of Great Russell Street) to St Pancras marked a distinct shift in the character of Bloomsbury. Scholars and their support network of bookshops and cafés were drawn northwards in its wake and over the last decade Bloomsbury has become less endearingly scruffy and more spruced up, like a cranky professor cajoled into a stiff new suit.

Change is inevitable, but it can be tricky to orchestrate the competing demands of tourists, students and residents. Museum Street, for instance, which used to house a lively assortment of book and print emporia, is now a sterile tourist trap. A rolling programme of landscape improvements to the major squares (Russell, Bloomsbury, Woburn and Gordon) has been well-intentioned and well-received, though implementing Humphry Repton's original (but never executed) layout of Bloomsbury Square might seem to have seriously denuded a once lush enclave.

The symbolic and literal epicentre of this area is still the British Museum – the first public museum in Europe, now dramatically remodelled by Foster

St Pancras Station, 1868-74, was once
threatened with demolition but has
now been restored to serve as London's
Eurostar terminus [Map p165 no.9]

and Partners to ease its sclerotic circulation and create a new public
gathering place. When the British Library moved to Camden in 1998
its book stacks, which occupied the quadrants around the famous Reading
Room, were demolished, and the glorious rotunda where Marx, Gandhi
and Kipling pored over their books was restored and opened to the public.

The surrounding space is enclosed by an undulating steel-and-glass
lattice roof and forms the new **Great Court**, Foster's modern version
of a winter garden, held within Robert Smirke's austere, Grecian embrace.
It improves circulation for the annual six million visitors, reveals the long-
hidden facades of the courtyard, and adds an elevated terrace restaurant.
Though the billowing glass roof looks effortless, it is actually a tour de force
of engineering by Buro Happold.

With its 'great estate' of academic buildings, **University College** is a key
player in both the historic and current evolution of Bloomsbury. Established
in 1828 for non-Anglican students (and so dubbed 'the godless college'),
it was the founding college of the University of London and also the first
to admit women as equals. Its oldest building is a domed central range at
the top end of Gower Street designed by William Wilkins, whose enthusiasm
for the radical Greek Revival style matched the progressive aims of the
institution. These aims are still manifest in an imaginative programme of
decent new buildings.

Notable among them is the **Brunei Gallery/SOAS Extension** by Nicholas
Hare Architects at the north-west corner of Russell Square, which completes
the square with a modern, mustard-brick facsimile of its late 18th-century
neighbours and then breaks away around the corner into something more
loose-limbed. Yet despite its assiduous attempts to be contexual, it is forced
to bear a plaque recording the fact that the University apparently failed to
consult the aristocratic Russell family on the design.

Close by, in Torrington Square, Stanton Williams play similar contextual
roulette at the **Clore Management Centre**, riffing and expounding more
adventurously on Georgian proportions and taking liberties with large areas
of glazing. Bolder still is Short & Associates' **School of Slavonic and Eastern
European Studies** in Taviton Street which brings a bracing whiff of the Baltic
to Bloomsbury, with brick walls the colour of dark rye bread. As part of
the ingenious mechanics of passive downdraught cooling, zinc-clad exhaust
stacks pepper the roof like robotic chess men.

In Gordon Street, Feilden Clegg Bradley's **Centre for Nanotechnology**
is a finely calculated response to a technically challenging brief, in which the
servicing required to provide a supremely uncontaminated research
environment accounted for over half the building budget. But there is poetry
too: the block of super-clean laboratories is wrapped in a delicate skin
of diaphanous steel mesh that creates gorgeous moiré effects, reflected in
mirror-clad window reveals.

The pivotal intersection of Gower Street and Euston Road is dominated
by a new complex for **University College Hospital** by Llewelyn Davies Yeang.
A tower and podium block are decked in layers of meringue-white cladding
interspersed with pistachio-green glazing, like a mammoth millefeuille.
A huge beaked entrance canopy, which probably looked better on the
visualisations, adds a sub-Calatrava flourish. It's a shame that such a major
project could not be a better advertisement for the dead hand of the Private

The generous courtyard of Colin St John Wilson's
British Library, 1978-97, built near St Pancras
after protests at two earlier proposals for a site
south of the British Museum [Map p165 no.22]

Foster and Partners' glazed Great Court at the
British Museum, 1994-2000, with the former Round
Reading Room at its centre [Map p167 no.17]

Short and Associates' School of Slavonic and East European Studies, 2005. The zinc-clad exhaust stacks on the roof are part of the ingenious cooling system [Map p167 no.53]

Feilden Clegg Bradley's Centre for
Nanotechnology, 2006, is clothed
in diaphanous steel mesh which creates
subtle visual effects [Map p167 no.56]

Feilden Clegg Bradley's Centre for
Nanotechnology with Fello Atkinson's
Bloomsbury Theatre, 1964-9,
on its left [Map p167 no.56 & no.38]

Terracotta louvres animate the
facade of Grimshaw's UCL Cancer
Institute, 2007 [Map p167 no.57]

Finance Initiative (PFI), but it did provide UCH with the opportunity to
re-evaluate its property holdings.

One outcome of this was the new **Cancer Institute** by Nicholas Grimshaw
on Huntley Street – a thoughtful piece of infill on a generally undistinguished
street, animated by a facade of vertical terracotta louvres. Each fin can be
rotated individually to create the illusion of a three-dimensional wave or,
more fancifully, a genetic bar code. The use of terracotta picks up on another
UCH landmark, Alfred Waterhouse's historic Cruciform Building on Gower
Street – the original hospital, now converted into teaching spaces.

In a further variation on a theme, Grimshaw is also responsible for the
Roberts Building on Torrington Place, a two-phase development to house
UCL's Engineering Faculty. The second part is now complete, veiled in
a crisply detailed facade of horizontal brises soleil.

Euston Road, London's great east-west artery, marks the northern extent
of Bloomsbury. It's a largely depressing thoroughfare, separating council
estates to the north (natural successors to the original workers' housing
crammed in between the railway lines) from the more coherent and historic
urban ensembles to the south. Along its car-choked length there is little to
cheer, but Michael Hopkins and Partners' **Gibbs Building** for the Wellcome
Trust has sufficient presence and that well-crafted, Jaguar-dashboard solidity
so characteristic of this practice.

Two blocks of unequal height and width frame a lofty atrium and though
it might sound formulaic, it isn't, with workers hanging out over the glazed
balustrades 'like residents in some aged Hong Kong apartment block,' says
Ken Allinson (in his *London's Contemporary Architecture*).

The west end of the atrium is further animated by Thomas Heatherwick's
Bleigeissen, a momumental installation modelled on how molten lead blobs
and swirls when dropped in water. In what must have been a mind-boggling
feat of assembly, it is created out of thousands of fist-sized 'beads' strung on
cables five storeys high.

Further east along Euston Road, set well back from its blare and bustle in
Flaxman Terrace is **The Place** dance school and performance venue by those
stalwarts of stealth Modernism, Allies and Morrison. A three-storey vitrine
offers tantalising glimpses of the building's inner life, as dancers prance,
preen and pose, silhouetted in the glass. Allies and Morrison have perfected
the art of nuanced understatement, which, unlike the output of some of their
flashier contemporaries, should stand the test of time. Their **City Lit** building
in Keeley Street, for instance, channels Alvar Aalto with gusto, enabling it to
take on some pretty meaty neighbours – the glowering temple of Freemasons
Hall and one of Richard Seifert's absurd circular office towers.

Bloomsbury's Georgian terraces and Victorian mansion blocks still provide
an adaptable template for modern living which has yet to be surpassed,
though there have been some flailing attempts. The most energetic of these
was Patrick Hodgkinson's **Brunswick Centre**, a prototypical megastructure
with Italian Futurist overtones intended to pioneer a high-density, low-rise
approach to city-centre dwelling. A pair of A-frames linked by raised decks
efficiently separated people and vehicles, creating a windswept axial
concourse surrounded by ziggurat-like terraces of apartments.

Now, in a major refurbishment programme overseen by Levitt Bernstein,
the concrete structure has been buffed and painted a dazzling Nash cream,

The Euston Road entrance to Michael Hopkins
and Partners' Gibbs Building for the Wellcome
Trust, 2005 [Map p167 no.54]

After being neglected for many years, Patrick Hodgkinson's Brunswick Centre, 1968-72, has recently been refurbished by Levitt Bernstein with Hodgkinson himself [Map p167 no.37]

Allies and Morrison's City Lit building, 2005, shows the influence of Alvar Aalto in its sweeping curves [Map p169 no.41]

MacCormac Jamieson Prichard's new
building for the BBC, begun in 2002,
distinctly echoes G Val Myers' Broadcasting
House, 1931 [Map p175 no.17]

'New headquarters for Ford Motors are tautly composed and elegantly executed, with a flourish of primary colours'

and the windows replaced. The Stalinist central allée has also been narrowed and made over to accommodate a parade of chi-chi shops, with the high temple of Waitrose at its northern extremity. Not quite the heroic brave new world of post-war imagination, but at least it speaks of an architecture robust enough to withstand the vicissitudes of physical and cultural reinvention.

Despite their colourful pasts, as havens respectively for artists and the sex industry, Fitzrovia and Soho are surprisingly fallow territory for contemporary architecture. Work is still in progress at **Broadcasting House** in Portland Place as the BBC grapples with remodelling and extending its famous 1930s premises to designs by MacCormac Jamieson Prichard. A new curved wing will be grafted on to the existing building forming a dialogue with both it and the historic pepper-pot of All Souls Church.

Deep in Fitzrovia's garment district, the **Sanderson** embodies a more challenging sort of historical dialogue. Originally built in the 1960s as offices for Sanderson wallpaper (with stained glass by John Piper), it is now the London flagship of Ian Schrager's boutique hotel empire. His house designer Philippe Starck turns his usual tricks with an eclectic bricolage of colour, texture and grotesque furniture, but the central courtyard, which has overtones of a Spanish patio garden, is actually rather delightful.

At least Starck has a kind of crazed but defiant vision, unlike the new building by Sheppard Robson for engineering giant **Arup** on Fitzroy Street, distinguished by what appears to be a huge green spider clinging to its facade, with fat silver ducts for legs.

Richard Rogers Partnership's **Ingeni** building in Broadwick Street shows how these things can be done. New headquarters for Ford Motors' creative department are tautly composed and elegantly executed with a flourish of High-Tech primary colours in the external lift-shaft.

Reprieved from swingeing development proposals in the 1970s, Covent Garden pioneered the template for heritage and shopping that has become the default setting for city centres everywhere. The **Royal Opera House** is still its most emblematic building, a ponderous Neo-Classical pile extended and animated by Dixon Jones in an exhaustive refurbishment programme.

Within, the ornately elegant auditorium with its Soanian saucer dome has been painstakingly renovated and the backstage areas greatly expanded. The Floral Hall – an airy, barrel-vaulted cast-iron and glass shed originally housing a flower market – has been transformed into the sumptuous main foyer, with restaurant and champagne bar. A mirrored wall gives the illusion of the original hall's eight bays, while making room for stage areas and workshops behind. A new arcade topped by a public loggia intelligently consolidates the urban form of Inigo Jones's square, while Wilkinson Eyre's ingenious corkscrew bridge links the main building with the ballet school on the north side, pirouetting coquettishly across the void.

The revitalisation of popular or grand institutions, adding to the sum of their parts and expanding their appeal, is a persistent theme. In the Piazza,

Richard Rogers Partnership's Ingeni building for
Derwent London, 1998-2000, is one of the few
new developments in Soho. Diagonally opposite
is a fine Georgian terrace [Map p173 no.34]

Avery Associates' refurbished **Transport Museum** in the shell of a 19th-century market building brings a cherished collection of models, posters and historical ephemera to life, complete with Routemaster cocktails, a homage to the late lamented bus. At **Somerset House** on the Strand, a grid of fountains and a winter ice rink have replaced parked cars in the handsome *cour d'honneur*, restored by Dixon Jones, and new galleries by Inskip + Jenkins in the south building house the Gilbert Collection of decorative arts. Formerly a staid and aloof home to the Navy and Tax offices, Somerset House is now a memorable addition to the public realm – its riverside terrace linked to Waterloo Bridge creating a new through route up to the Strand.

Dixon Jones seem to haunt this part of London, but in an entirely benign way. Their East Wing and Central Portico projects for the **National Gallery** rationalise circulation and create an elegant new set of interiors, while next door at the **National Portrait Gallery** new galleries in the Ondaatje Wing are deftly slotted into the existing fabric around a soaring, vertiginous void. The top floor houses the Portrait Restaurant, a long, thin utilitarian room with spectacular Mary Poppins views of the London skyline.

From here you can survey **Trafalgar Square**, now elevated from its status of glorified traffic island to what passes for a piazza in London. In a Byzantinely intricate feat of traffic engineering, Foster and Partners and Atkins' re-planning involved closing off the north side to form a new pedestrian promenade in front of the National Gallery. New steps connect this terrace with the square, and though some critics argue that this has unbalanced the overall proportions, the experiential benefits of traffic banishment are palpable.

On the east side of the square James Gibbs' church of **St Martin-in-the-Fields** (originally thought 'a little too gay and theatrical for Protestant worship') continues its historic mission of social and cultural welfare, newly reinvigorated by a major development programme overseen by Eric Parry Architects, and a fitting point to conclude this trajectory of notable new and recent architecture.

From the back streets of King's Cross to the civic heart of Trafalgar Square, it is clear that London is an extraordinarily complex and still-evolving mosaic. Forming and reforming over time, it democratically embraces both the grungy and the grand, and this latest wave of development is proof, if it were needed, of the city's enduring capacity to reinvent itself.

Catherine Slessor is an architectural journalist and managing editor of the Architectural Review

Dixon Jones has refurbished and extended
the Royal Opera House in Covent Garden,
consolidating the form of Inigo Jones' Piazza
[Map p169 no.15]

Portfolio
A Sense Of Place

Photography by Dominik Gigler

Broadcasting House by G Val Myers, 1931
[Map p175 no.17]

Sicilian Avenue by R J Worley, 1905-10
[Map p169 no.25]

New Zealand House by RMJM, 1957-63
[Map p173 no.31]

Woburn Walk by Thomas Cubitt,
c.1822 [Map p167 no.16]

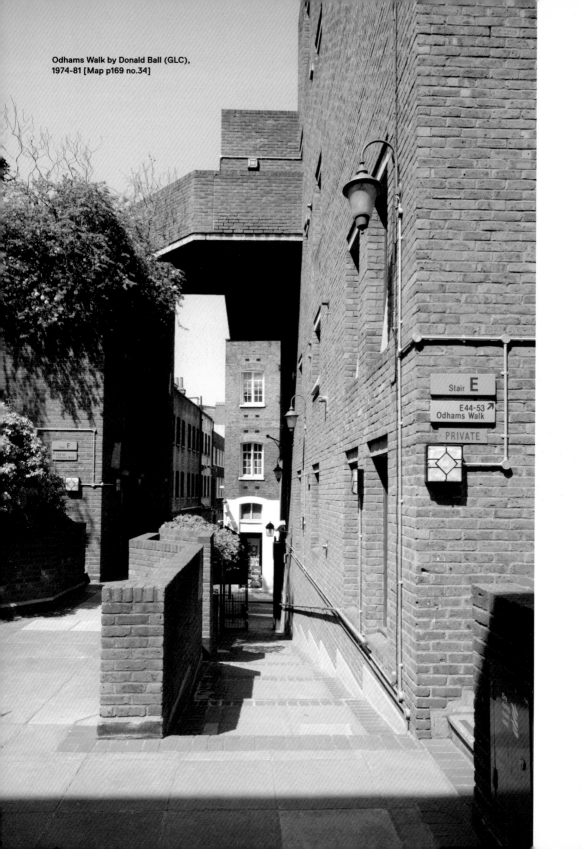

Odhams Walk by Donald Ball (GLC),
1974-81 [Map p169 no.34]

Waterloo Place with the United Service
Club by John Nash, 1826-8, and the
Athenaeum by Decimus Burton, 1827-30
[Map p173 no.13 & no.14]

Congress House by David du R Aberdeen,
1953-7 [Map p167 no.35]

48-58 Broadwick Street, 1722-3
[Map p173 no.4]

All Souls School by A Beresford Pite,
1906-8 [Map p175 no.13]

St George, Bloomsbury Way, by Nicholas Hawksmoor, 1716-31 [Map p167 no.2]

Chandos House by Robert Adam, 1769-71 [Map p175 no.3]

All Saints, Margaret Street, by William Butterfield, 1849-59 [Map p175 no.8]

YMCA Indian Student Hostel by
Ralph Tubbs, 1952 [Map p175 no.20]

The Place by Allies and Morrison, 2001
[Map p167 no.51]

Goodwin's Court, late 18th century
[Map p169 no.12]

St Pancras New Church by H W & W
Inwood, 1819-22 [Map p167 no.14]

James Smith's umbrella shop, c.1870
[Map p169 no.20]

Mary Ward House by A Dunbar Smith
and Cecil Brewer, 1895-7 [Map p167 no.22]

Gagosian Gallery by
Caruso St John, 2003–4
[Map p165 no.26]

PCL School of Engineering & Science by Lyons,
Israel & Ellis, 1965–8 [Map p175 no.23]

Burberry's by Walter Cave, 1911-13
[Map p173 no.24]

Candover Street housing
by H Fuller Clark, 1903
[Map p175 no.12]

Ossulston Estate by G Topham Forrest (LCC),
1927-31 [Map p165 no 17]

All Souls, Langham Place, by John Nash,
1822-4 [Map p175 no.7]

Fire Station by LCC Fire Brigade Branch, 1901-2 [Map p165 no.14]

The Salisbury, 1898
[Map p169 no.22]

Constructing
The Future

This section presents masterplans that are meant
to guide development and some major projects
that are now under way. It is a taste of things
to come – with the proviso that the future of these
areas does not depend on high-profile schemes
alone but on well-judged small-scale interventions

Masterplans

King's Cross

Masterplanner: Allies & Morrison,
Porphyrios Associates
Client: Argent Group PLC and London
& Continental Railways, DHL-Exel

Formerly a depressed inner city area with
decaying fabric, social problems and vast tracts
of inhospitable industrial land, King's Cross is
now one of the most significant development
and regeneration opportunities in central
London. Outline planning permission for the
67 acre site around the station was granted
in December 2006 for nearly 8 million sq ft
of new mixed-use development. The plans are
ambitious, including up to 25 new office
buildings, 20 new streets, 10 new major public
spaces, the restoration and refurbishment of
20 historic buildings and structures, and some
2,000 homes and serviced apartments. The
area will also host new theatres, independent
cinemas, exhibition spaces and community
facilities which will mesh with an already thriving
local arts scene. In addition Central Saint
Martins, part of London's University of the Arts,
will relocate to the Eastern Goods Yard, bringing
5,000 students into the area.

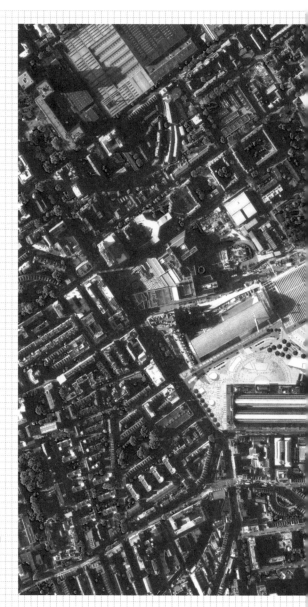

ROYAL OAK
Study for key pedestrian
movement areas beneath
Westway needed

UPPER EDGWARE RD.
IMPACT STUDY AND
SECTION 106
Improvements associated
with redevelopment
proposals

WESTMINSTER
UNIVERSITY/ MADAME
TUSSAUDS BAKER ST.
Combined study for shared
public realm areas required

Study initiated by
ROYAL ACADEMY OF
MUSIC
for public realm and private
frontage areas by
Munckenbeck & Marshall

PRINCE OF WALES
JUNCTION
Local action has initiated
calls for a pedestrian plan at
road junctions on Harrow
Road

Concept stage ideas for
'GREEN BRIDGE'
linking Paddington Green
to Basin across Westway

LISSON GROVE/ CHURCH
ST. WARD
Urban design and housing
studies by Westminster City
Council Housing
Department

Regent's Park

REGENTS
PARK
ESTATE

SOMERS TO

CHURCH ST WARD &
LISSON GROVE ESTATES

WARWICK AVENUE/
PADDINGTON GREEN

PADDINGTON STATION,
PADDINGTON BASIN,
GOODS YARD
Public realm improvements
to include pedestrian and
road changes below West-
way connecting Maida Vale/
Little Venice to Paddington
Basin

PRIORITY PROJECT
for new intersection
modelled on ongoing
Euston Road/ Tottenham
Court Road project

Ongoing creation of
MARYLEBONE HIGH ST.
as London's best by
Howard de Walden Estate

BLOOMSB

LOWER EDGWARE RD.
ACTION PLAN
Street improvements by
Westminster City Council

AIR RIGHTS AND LINKING
OF BOTH EDGWARE RD.
TUBE STATIONS
Study required by TFL/
WCC that extends to
pedestrian crossings at
Landmark Hotel frontages

FARRELLS

MARYLEBONE / EUSTON RD: NOT AN URBAN MOTORWAY BUT LONDON'S 'MAIN
SUMMARY PLAN OF PROGRESS ON MARYLEBONE ROAD SECTION

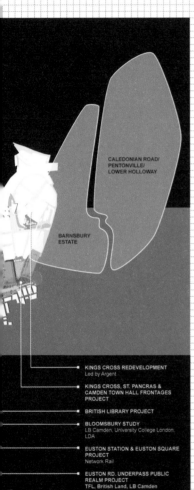

BARNSBURY
ESTATE

CALEDONIAN ROAD/
PENTONVILLE/
LOWER HOLLOWAY

'REET'

- **KINGS CROSS REDEVELOPMENT**
  Led by Argent

- **KINGS CROSS, ST. PANCRAS &
  CAMDEN TOWN HALL FRONTAGES
  PROJECT**

- **BRITISH LIBRARY PROJECT**

- **BLOOMSBURY STUDY**
  LB Camden, University College London,
  LDA

- **EUSTON STATION & EUSTON SQUARE
  PROJECT**
  Network Rail

- **EUSTON RD. UNDERPASS PUBLIC
  REALM PROJECT**
  TFL, British Land, LB Camden

- **HOLY TRINITY CHURCH
  ENVIRONMENTAL IMPROVEMENT
  PROJECT**
  British Land

- **NASH RAMBLAS**
  Steering group: project managed by CLP
  in conjunction with
  English Heritage, Farrells, Crown Estate,
  New West End Company, Future London,
  Royal Parks Agency, Crown Estates
  Paving Commission, London Borough of
  Camden, London Borough of Westminster,
  BBC, Heart of London Business Alliance,
  Howard de Walden Estate, London Zoo,
  Great Portland Estate, Transport for
  London, Langham Hotel, University of
  Westminster, CABE, GLA

Marylebone/ Euston Road

Masterplanner: Farrells
Client: GLA

Though it is currently a busy, blaring traffic artery, Marylebone-Euston Road has the potential to become one of London's greatest assets with street life, landscaping, major squares and green spaces. Farrells are engaged in a series of linked masterplanning studies for areas on or around the road. These include Nash Ramblas (an axial north-south route from Primrose Hill to South Bank), the Royal Academy of Music frontage, the Westway, Tottenham Circus and the frontages of King's Cross and St Pancras. Farrells' framework has acted as a catalyst for change. A key aspect of the masterplan is a detailed design study of Euston Circus (above), where Tottenham Court Road meets Euston Road, which aims to civilise this key junction as a pedestrian-friendly connection between Fitzrovia and the more marginalised areas to the north.

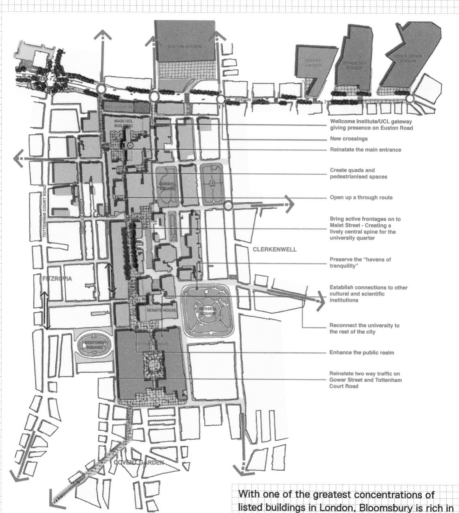

Wellcome Institute/UCL gateway giving presence on Euston Road

New crossings

Reinstate the main entrance

Create quads and pedestrianised spaces

Open up a through route

Bring active frontages on to Malet Street - Creating a lively central spine for the university quarter

Preserve the "havens of tranquility"

Establish connections to other cultural and scientific institutions

Reconnect the university to the rest of the city

Enhance the public realm

Reinstate two way traffic on Gower Street and Tottenham Court Road

Masterplans

Bloomsbury

Masterplanner: Farrells
Client: London Borough of Camden, University College London and London Development Agency

With one of the greatest concentrations of listed buildings in London, Bloomsbury is rich in architecture, squares and heritage. To enhance this precious but in parts neglected public realm, the London Borough of Camden – in partnership with UCL and the London Development Agency – commissioned Farrells to develop a framework document to guide future development. Now Camden is taking the first steps to implement the vision. New schemes are proposed for Great Russell Street and Montague Place, along with streetscape improvements on Malet Street and a new public square at Byng Place.

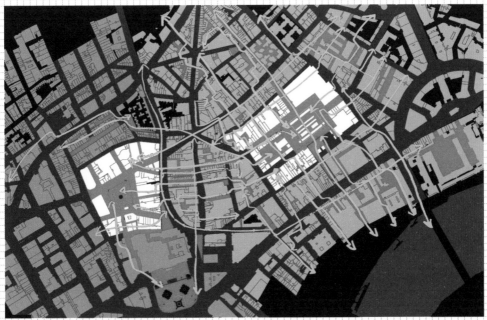

Masterplans

Covent Garden

Masterplanner: Kohn Pedersen Fox
Client: Capco Covent Garden

As London's oldest public square Covent Garden Piazza has great civic, historic and commercial importance, yet today it is a congested and uninspiring tourist trap. Plans to revive the area focus on retaining its positive physical and social attributes while differentiating it from all the UK high streets it now seems to resemble – and thereby reinforcing its status as a key retail and cultural destination. Masterplanner Kohn Pedersen Fox says the main challenge is to respect Covent Garden's heritage while ensuring it meets the needs of a modern and inclusive urban centre. KPF seeks to improve legibility and permeability throughout the Covent Garden area with a mix of public realm improvements and building redevelopment. It aims to create more opportunities for people to relax or be a spectator in a district that at present is dominated by crowds thronging the streets. It also highlights routes through some lesser-known passageways and courtyards.

Masterplans

Fitzrovia

Masterplanner: Farrells
Client: LMS

Farrells carried out a study to examine future options for Fitzrovia, defined by Tottenham Court Road to the east, Great Portland Street to the west, Euston Road to the north and Oxford Street to the south. Part of the brief was to establish a synergy between movement, highway design, public space and landscape. Farrells' proposals aim to improve connections to surrounding neighbourhoods by creating a network of upgraded pedestrian routes and 'pocket' parks, together with better public transport access. The plans also seek to make Fitzrovia a distinctive urban quarter, broken down into a series of individual neighbourhoods.

Uses at Ground Floor Level

- Retail
- Residential
- Hospitality (Bars, Cafés, Restaurants)
- Recreation and Leisure (Gyms etc)
- Office (all types)
- Civic
- Health (Hospitals, Surgery, Dental etc)
- Education (Schools, Universities etc)
- Tourism
- Ecclesiastic
- Government (Embassies)
- Media
- Financial (Banks, Post Offices etc)
- Arts (Theatre, Galleries etc)

Masterplans

Crossrail

Client: Cross London Rail Links

Improvements to Tottenham Court Road underground station have been urgently needed for some time, and the go-ahead for Crossrail (the new east-west route across London) has been the spur for development. Tottenham Court Road station will be effectively rebuilt, giving access to both Crossrail and the Central line. There will be a new western entrance from Dean Street in Soho, while the eastern end, served by a new ticket hall, will have remodelled entrances at the south-west and north-east corners of St Giles Circus. As well as responding to the needs of an increasing number of passengers, the work will make access to the station easier, with improvements to the existing Oxford St/Charing Cross Road junction.

Projects

King's Cross Station

Architect: John McAslan + Partners
Client: Network Rail

Due to be complete in 2012, King's Cross Station is currently undergoing an extensive programme of restoration and modernisation overseen by John McAslan + Partners. As well as infrastructural improvements, the station itself will be enhanced by the addition of a new concourse on its west side, enclosed by a dramatic curved-glass canopy that radiates out from a central vortex. Removal of the existing single-storey addition on the main frontage will once again expose the magnificent muscularity of Lewis Cubitt's double vaults and create a new public square for King's Cross.

Projects

St Pancras Chambers

Architect: RHWL Architects
Client: Manhattan Loft Corporation
and London & Continental Railways

At the turn of the 20th century, the High Victorian Gothic masterpiece of George Gilbert Scott's Midland Hotel was the most luxurious establishment in Europe, but it has lain empty for many years and came close to demolition in the 1960s, when Victorian excess was being ritually purged by zealous Modernists. Now the wheel has come full circle and ornateness is back in favour, so Manhattan Loft Corporation has begun a £150 million investment programme that will see the ultimate luxury hotel reborn once more. Five stars, 245 rooms, 68 apartments, a ballroom, business centre, bars and restaurants will all be in place by 2010.

Projects

Kings Place

Architect: Dixon Jones
Client: Parabola Land

Lying between York Way and the canal basin is the Kings Place development by Dixon Jones. This seven-storey building is more than an office block, for it contains a new 420-seat concert hall that will be a permanent home for the Orchestra of the Age of Enlightenment and the London Sinfonietta. There will also be a gallery for the Borchard Collection of British Self-Portraits, a sculpture space, and a restaurant overlooking Battlebridge canal basin. Initial tenants will be the Guardian newspaper, defecting north from Clerkenwell to help spearhead the King's Cross renaissance.

Projects

Regent's Place

Architect: Arup Associates,
Farrells, Sheppard Robson, Wilkinson Eyre
Client: British Land

The masterplan for the western quarter of Regent's Place was conceived in the context of Farrells' Euston-Marylebone Study, which seeks to challenge the view that the road is a lifeless thoroughfare. The big move here is the creation of a new east-west route, forming a pedestrian link with shops between Regent's Park and Drummond Street. Five new buildings are planned in two phases, with Farrells designing three schemes along Osnaburgh Street, including the first residential development in Regent's Place. This will comprise 151 private, intermediate and affordable homes, and a 21-storey residential tower to take advantage of views over nearby Regent's Park. Proposals also include around 362,000 sq ft of office space, specifically targeted at the West End market.

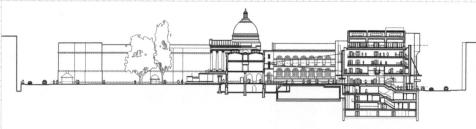

Projects

Institute for Cultural Heritage, UCL

Architect: Dixon Jones
Client: University College London

Following a competition, a scheme by Dixon Jones was selected to house the University's Rare Books and Manuscripts Collection and its Egyptian treasure trove, the Petrie Collection. The Gordon Street site is important both for its urban context and its significance in the overall layout of UCL. As well as creating a building of interest both to the university community and the wider public – 'UCL's window on the world, and the world's window into UCL' – the project identifies a horizontal route that connects Gordon Street to the front quadrangle, the historic main entrance to the college. The relationship between the two sides of UCL's city block will at last become clear.

Leicester Square

Architect: Burns + Nice
Client: City of Westminster

Leicester Square, first known as Leicester Fields, dates back to 1670 – it was among the earliest developments as London expanded westwards beyond the confines of the City. It lost its social cachet in the mid-19th century and became instead a focus of entertainment. Today it is seen as the 'home of British cinema', a place of premieres, but with little allure in itself. Initiated by Westminster City Council and supported by the Heart of London Business Alliance and the Leicester Square Association, work is now underway to upgrade the square and its environs. A landscape design competition in 2007 was won by Burns + Nice in conjunction with DPA Lighting, and their scheme addresses the square, the garden at its centre, and the streets that cement it into the West End. It includes new water features, new seating (flexible where possible) and enhanced lighting, as well as the removal of some current clutter, both physical and visual. Westminster hopes the revitalised square will be 'the West End's principal meeting place'.

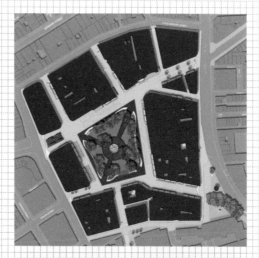

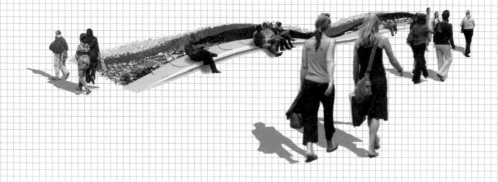

Projects

Central St Giles

Architect: Renzo Piano
Client: Legal & General
and Mitsubishi Estate Company

Designed by Renzo Piano, this vast mixed-use
development will recast and rehabilitate St Giles
High Street – the site of Hogarth's infamous Gin
Lane in the 18th century and faring little better
in the 20th, beset as it is by traffic congestion
and general urban squalor. Statistically,
the scheme is impressive, with 375,000 sq ft
of office space, 56 private apartments and
53 affordable homes, plus the familiar mélange
of restaurants and shops at ground level. It
also involves the creation of new access routes
across the site together with a public courtyard
at Princes Circus. Architecturally, it is slightly
formulaic Piano, with angular facades wrapped
in glass and terracotta, but it's a distinct
improvement on the glum Orwellian compound
of government offices it will replace.

Projects

Silken Hotel

Architect: Foster and Partners
Client: Grupo Urvasco S.A.

Located on a plum site at the intersection of
the Strand and the Aldwych, this new five-star
hotel by Foster and Partners is the first UK
venture for the Spanish Silken Hotel Group.
Within a resonantly historic location (its near
neighbours include India House and Bush House),
Foster combines the restored listed facade
of Marconi House with a new building clad in
Portland stone (in keeping with the original
Aldwych masterplan) and an entirely restructured
interior. The scheme comprises restaurants,
bars, a panoramic rooftop terrace, 170 bedrooms
and 90 apartments. A soaring, eleven-storey
atrium adds to the sense of theatre.

Projects

Fitzrovia Apartments

Architect: Make
Client: Manhattan Loft Corporation
& Ridgeford Properties

Historically a home to bohemians and artists, Fitzrovia is slowly re-emerging as a fashionable city centre address. New apartments by HOK for the Manhattan Loft Corporation and Ridgeford Properties in Bolsover Street will doubtless add to its cosmopolitan allure. As part of the deal, the National Orthopaedic Hospital will gain new facilities, with the surrounding land developed to accommodate 66 apartments and a quartet of luxury penthouses, together with an element of affordable housing and a small office development in an existing listed building.

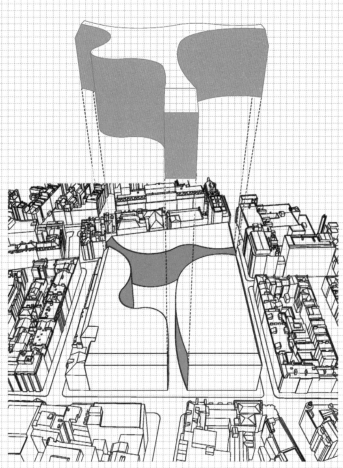

Projects

Noho Square

Architect: Make
Client: Candy & Candy

Since the 1920s the red brick behemoth of Middlesex Hospital has loomed over north Fitzrovia. In 2005 it finally closed and the Mortimer Street site was sold off to fund the redevelopment of University College Hospital on Euston Road. Now the site is being ambitiously redeveloped to designs by Ken Shuttleworth's practice Make and branded as Noho Square. A trio of apartment blocks with fashionably rippling facades will enclose a new public garden. The divisions between the buildings extend adjoining streets as routes into the garden, where the hospital's listed Victorian Gothic chapel will be preserved.

The NLA Sky Walk

For the London Festival of Architecture 2008,
New London Architecture asked Carmody Groarke
to create a temporary structure in Montague Place,
a neglected street beside the British Museum

Peter Murray, director of the London Festival of Architecture, explains how the NLA Sky Walk reflects a fundamental concept of the festival

I cycle through Montague Place several times every day. It is a nondescript part of the city despite the fact that it sits behind the greatest repository of cultural artefacts in the western world, links two fine squares, and is adjacent to Charles Holden's dramatic Senate House.

For a long time I didn't take much notice of the space. I dodged the coaches as they unloaded tourists, the other cyclists who pack Camden's over-protective cycle route that runs right down the centre of it, and wondered about the curious caravan café that sits incongruously outside the north entrance to the British Museum.

It was after Terry Farrell announced his masterplan for Bloomsbury and revealed the potential of Montague Place that I started to get angry when I cycled through it. Here was a potentially elegant public square, accessing a very public building, that was being treated like a supermarket car park. The traffic engineers and the parking department hold sway here.

At the British Museum, Foster and Partners not only opened up the magnificent Great Court but provided a north-south route right through the centre of the building, changing for ever the dynamics of the area. Connect that inspired move with Transport for London's efforts to promote walking; with the museum's plans by Rogers Stirk Harbour to redevelop the north-west side of the building; with the thousands of tourists arriving at St Pancras Station who will cross Russell Square, and vainly try to find the entrance to the museum. Connect all these things together and you know that Montague Place will have to change.

The Sky Walk by Carmody Groarke is designed to help us see – to understand the space in a different way and to inspire ideas for its future use. When people taste its potential they will no longer be satisfied that such a dull and second-rate place sits within the network of wonderful Georgian squares of Bloomsbury. The Sky Walk reinforces a fundamental concept of the Festival of Architecture – that by understanding the city, we can see its potential and change it for the better.

Kevin Carmody and **Andy Groarke** of Carmody Groarke describe the strategy behind their intervention

The basis for our architectural installation within Montague Place was a consideration of public space – and spaces for activity – instead of the spectacle of an 'object' pavilion itself.

By breaking down its scale into a series of smaller, public event and exhibition spaces, this broad street can host a programme of continuous and simultaneous activities. Our strategy for enclosing these places finally took the form of a 160m-long ramped wall, scissoring back and forth across the street and topped with an 'inhabited walkway' linking Malet Street at its west end with Russell Square at the east.

The walkway is built from a hardwearing but simple and efficient portable staging system – not just for speed of construction, but so that as much material as possible from this temporary structure can be readily re-used in the future. Its walls are then covered in a translucent black mesh fabric to reinforce the installation's sculptural quality. While the spaces and their use change through the three-day programme, the mesh creates an intriguing moiré effect and a constant visual link between adjacent activities, as well as a surface for exhibition narrative and interpretation.

Consistent with the events-based nature of the installation – rather like a temporary theatre or rock concert stage – it is meant to provide a simple, provisional structure for observing and participating in the activities and events of the festival. As such the installation is just a framework for the activity, not the generator.

While giving elevated views of the northern entrance to the British Museum and adjacent Georgian squares, this temporary promenade also creates an unexpected change of pace and new perspectives of Montague Place, by offering ways to explore the structure at various levels. The shape and profile of the route is composed around – and positively affected by – existing features within the street, whether focusing on the northern entrance of the museum or making a performance stage planted around the trunk of a London Plane tree.

Above all, the short life of this festival installation in Montague Place gives visitors a chance to think about urban design. It heightens awareness of the architecture, landscape and details of an urban environment that is otherwise disregarded day-to-day.

Kevin Carmody and Andrew Groarke established Carmody Groarke in 2006. Their studio was named Young Architect of the Year in 2007 and is currently working on diverse projects in the UK and abroad

Jonathan Stock and **Debbie Whitfield**
from NLA give the client's perspective
on this ambitious project

Montague Place was always our starting point.
Bordered by Senate House and the British
Museum, it is at the centre of the capital's cultural
and academic heart, linking Bedford and Russell
Squares – two fine examples of landscaping and
green public space. But as a street or public space
in its own right, it seems to be totally overlooked.
Pedestrians routinely ask passers-by for directions
to the museum while standing seconds from its
underused north entrance.

In the spirit of the festival, the street presented
an opportunity to take a fairly unknown part of
central London and showcase its potential to
become one of the capital's great public spaces.
We were aware that the museum had already seen
an opportunity for change here as part of its
development plans, where the construction of
Rogers Stirk Harbour's new conservation centre
will impact on Montague Place.

Working with Carmody Groarke allowed us
to make the potential of Montague Place tangible.
The practice had shown its ability to transform
public space sensitively but powerfully with its
competition-winning Osnaburgh Pavilion at
Regent's Place for British Land, and it understood
the opportunity here immediately.

Our loose brief was to create something that,
although provisional in nature, would allow for
a new perspective of the street and provide spaces
that could be activated during the NLA festival
programme. Carmody Groarke's response was
an 'anti-pavilion': a structure that stretched our
expectations through its scale but with a
refreshingly anti-ego approach at its core.

Our aim is that the NLA Sky Walk's existence
over just three days in July 2008 will be much
more than an ephemeral event. The festival
performances and exhibitions that occupy it will
be significant, rooted as they are in the people,
institutions and architecture of the area of London
it sits in. But we hope it will also create a
sufficiently memorable image that will reverberate
in people's minds – a 'palpable ghost' raising
issues about how you can analyse, reformulate
and use open spaces and parts of the city.

An immense amount of work was put in by a hugely dedicated project team to make the NLA Sky Walk possible. NLA would like to thank in particular: Kevin Carmody, Andy Groarke and Berit Bessell, Carmody Groarke; Richard Howey, Steeldeck; William Whitby, Arup; Piers Roberts, Designersblock; Jack Tilbury, Charcoal Blue; Bob West, Piers Masterson, John Futcher and Robert Slaney, London Borough of Camden; the British Museum team

Sightlines

A collection of personal insights into
King's Cross, Bloomsbury, Covent Garden,
Holborn, Soho & Fitzrovia

Dan Cruickshank...

hopes the Euston Arch will soon be rebuilt

The Euston Arch, completed in 1838, was the first great monument of the railway age and formed the entry to London's Euston Station, the first main line terminus in the world. The arch marked the point of departure from London to the north for all using the new wonder of the age – the railway. It was the largest Doric propylaeum (or gateway) ever built and one of the finest examples of Greek Revival architecture in Europe or America (see page 017).

Its architect Philip Hardwick had created one of the most visually powerful and symbolic monuments of the 19th century. It was a masterpiece; not least because of the ingenuity of its engineered structure, in which the arch's gritstone blocks were no more than a cladding over a relatively lightweight iron, timber and brick-built frame.

During the 1930s British Railways announced its intention to rebuild Euston Station but – as was only civilised – the arch was to be preserved. The war delayed the redevelopment until the late 1950s; but now, in an age brutalised by destruction, there was a vital difference of intention. British Railways no longer wanted to go to the trouble or expense of preserving the arch.

This provoked a mighty battle between the forces of conservation and those of crudely-envisaged 'progress' – but in 1962 the arch was demolished. As it turned out, though, it was gone but not obliterated. In the early 1990s a search was launched for its stones that were rumoured to have been saved by the demolition contractor. Some were found in his garden in Bromley, Kent, but the vast majority had been tipped into the Prescott Channel, that runs into the River Lea in east London. Around 60% has now been located of the 4,450 tons of stone used in the construction of the arch.

With Euston Station due for redevelopment yet again – scheduled to start in 2012 – a campaign has been launched to rebuild the arch at Euston using a large proportion of salvaged original stone. The rebuilt arch would not be a pastiche but a largely authentic construction, a heroic piece of repair. Doing this would not only right a great wrong and reveal that beauty can be brought back from the grave but would also give the new Euston Station distinction, history and character. It could possess some of the quality that the public much enjoys at the recently restored St Pancras Station, in which exemplary modern design is integrated happily with the best of Victorian railway architecture.

The campaign is being headed by the Euston Arch Trust (EAT) and has the support of English Heritage, local MP Frank Dobson and Terry Farrell, who has drawn up a masterplan for the Euston Road. The project is affordable and feasible – it's now up to Londoners, and all interested in history, beauty and culturally rich contemporary architecture, to fight to get the arch back. If all work together, the arch could be reborn. At Euston beauty and delight, not philistinism, should have the last word.

Dan Cruickshank is an architectural historian and broadcaster.
For more information about the campaign visit www.eustonarch.org

Benedict O'Looney...
relishes some Edwardian buildings

I decided to become an architect because I believed that architecture brought together all the arts: painting, sculpture, and building. I loved to draw and pursuing architecture seemed to bring all I was interested together in one undertaking: line, sculptural mass, materials, colour, detail. Often today one loses sight of the power of this fusion of the arts, but in London's Edwardian architecture, this dream seems very much realised – a delight and a continual inspiration for me.

These buildings still seem so useful and relevant because their architects pursued a free, innovative bent – looking out beyond past traditions to find an architecture appropriate and stimulating for a new century. The designers I am interested in – Treadwell and Martin, Beresford Pite, H Fuller Clark, Lanchester and Rickards, and many others – were all much inspired by the continental Art Nouveau. Britain's distinctive Arts and Crafts movement also fed into this adventurous tendency, with its emphasis on honesty and clarity in detailing and the happy integration of the different building crafts.

Often these buildings are tucked away on side streets, away from the more predictable commercial architecture of London's high streets. Treadwell and Martin specialized in maximising density for developers on the narrow sites of Georgian houses, which were being pulled down all over the West End in the years around 1900 as their leases expired. See their lovely Rising Sun pub on the corner of Tottenham Court Road and Windmill Street (pictured left), or the sensuous Art Nouveau profiles of their Old Shades pub on Whitehall.

Another favourite architect of mine whose buildings offer a range of lessons in brickwork detailing is Beresford Pite. A brilliant draftsman, Pite contributed to some of London's finest fin de siècle building in partnership with the established architect John Belcher. On his own, however, after 1897, Pite created a series of strikingly modern buildings in the streets of Fitzrovia. Check out the inexpensive but amusing polychrome brick detailing and lovely lettering on his All Souls School at Foley Street and Cleveland Street. This polychrome spirit is also in evidence at the spunky 21 Little Portland Street and at the former women's hostel at 44 Mortimer Street.

The apotheosis of this Edwardian search for a new decorative language in architecture and its synthesis with sculpture can be seen at Alfred Gilbert's Shaftesbury memorial in Piccadilly Circus. I never tire of looking at this: it is intricate, organic, beautiful and a tour-de force of craftsmanship. Golly, could these designers draw and model – what confidence they had!

Benedict O'Looney is a partner in Morris + O'Looney Architects and teaches history and sketching at Canterbury School of Architecture

Simon Silver...

stresses the need for sensitive development in Fitzrovia

Fitzrovia is a unique place in London. In the heart of the West End, it sits between the estates of Marylebone and Bloomsbury, yet it has a different feel altogether – it's one of London's hidden gems. Unlike those neighbouring villages, its architectural grain is a direct result of diverse and fragmented ownership over the centuries, which today is central to its very character.

Derwent London now has a large number of holdings in the area and, as an active manager of the estate, will be maintaining, improving, and sometimes redeveloping the buildings. We have a design-led attitude and use good contemporary architects who are as passionate about design as we are. This not only applies to the buildings themselves, but also to the street scene. Fitzrovia has a number of open spaces such as Whitfield Gardens which are screaming out for attention. There is also an accidental open space in Goodge Street – a missing tooth that will be redeveloped before long.

Our approach is very much to enhance and maintain the area's vibrant community, ensuring any new development harmonises and meshes with the existing. But above all to celebrate its sense of place and invest in opportunities, like enlivening street frontages with retail. I would like to see this done sensitively and sustainably, so that future generations in Fitzrovia will recognise its eras of architecture, including today's, with equal affection.

Simon Silver is head of development at Derwent London

Alan Rusbridger...

anticipates the Guardian's move to King's Cross

The corner of Goods Way and York Road near the back of King's Cross station is an unlovely spot. For years it was enlivened by a piece of graffiti recording that 'the DPP crawled here'. It was a dark, neglected Victorian corner where Londoners could – and regularly did – meet ladies of the night in comparative obscurity (until the Director of Public Prosecutions, but that's another story).

The BP petrol station and the neglected wastes of the old gas works are still not beautiful. But look around and some wonderful things are happening. To the west is the sleek new concrete and glass St Pancras Station and to the east the rather extraordinary wave of dark glass which cloaks the Guardian's new home.

Called Kings Place, it has been designed by Dixon Jones for an enlightened developer who has subverted the idea of the traditional speculation. In addition to seven floors of office space, half of which we will occupy, the building has a beautiful 420-seat concert hall, two resident orchestras – The Age of Enlightenment and the Sinfonietta – as well as sculpture and art galleries and a restaurant. The wave of glass, which subtly echoes the waterside location, is in fact an ingenious triple façade which deflects solar gain in summer and insulates the building in winter. When we made the decision to move, we looked at more than 20 different developments in and around central London, and this was by far the most considered.

Walk down the steps opposite the BP station and head towards Islington. Round the back of the Guardian's new building the waterway opens out into the glorious Battlebridge Basin on Regent's Canal. In two minutes you're in the lower reaches of the Caledonian Road. Within 10 years the land on the other side of York Way will have developed beyond all recognition: a giant 67 acre site owned by Argent, which will include the campus for the University of the Arts. With the Kings Place concert hall, the British Library to the south and Antony Gormley's studio to the north, the area will be a fascinating artistic hub.

Other papers have headed for the towers of Canary Wharf or the shopping havens of Kensington. King's Cross feels right for the Guardian – a move ahead of its time, a little edgy, and a fascinating community all around.

Alan Rusbridger is Editor of the Guardian

Stephanie Macdonald...
observes daily life in Holborn

Sometimes I swim in the open air hidden from the traffic by high-rise.

My nine-year-old can go to Coram Fields with his friends by himself but I can't go without him.

It takes three minutes to walk to work if I go the long way.

The brick wall in our courtyard has a small stone inlaid dated 1708; it says Bedford Bounde. Above it is a decayed enamelled metal plaque that says Rugby Estate 1824.

Sir John Soane's Museum has the best Piranesis but you need to know which panels they are hidden behind.

When I wanted a piano I found that Conway Hall held piano auctions.

On Friday mornings before school we go to La Provence for breakfast (in Gray's Inn Road).

Why does the tall Georgian terrace on Great Ormond Street have just one house painted blue? I like it. I wouldn't like more than one.

Could the vaults under Lambs Conduit Street be used for something?

The man with a van of liquid nitrogen for the School of Pharmacy used to make clouds and ice puddles for Laurie on the way to nursery school.

I was sad when they re-laid the stone flags on the little square on Rugby Street with 50mm cement joints instead of 3mm silver sand.

Kennards on Lambs Conduit Street is the source of delicious food, neighbourhood introductions and general wellbeing.

Sometimes we play tennis at Lincoln's Inn Fields at 8am on Sunday and then get fresh croissants on the way back.

Sometimes I go to the bookshop at the Architectural Association and read what I like.

Sometimes I hear eight languages being spoken in our studio.

I love living in Holborn but sometimes I don't. It can make me lazy.

Stephanie Macdonald is a partner in 6a Architects. Her thoughts on Holborn were inspired by Georges Perec's 'On the Difficulty of Imagining an Ideal City'

Mark Whitby...
believes Fitzrovia is still bohemian – but only just

I arrived in Fitzrovia 35 years ago, and, for me it is as much a spiritual home as the Strumble in west Wales. Though the delicatessens and the art shop Tiranti's have gone, the Curwen Gallery and the Newman Arms are just as they ever were – although a John Piper and a pint are now a little more expensive.

Restaurants seem noisier and Anna from Bertorelli's is no longer with us. Gone are the stories that Anna or Sir Alan Harris (the boss at Harris and Sutherland) told of Ove Arup. The traffic, thanks to Ken Livingstone, is calmer but the road surface just as unreliable for cyclists.

This is London's engineering quarter, where the profession decamped from Victoria when it no longer needed to be close to Parliament. It is also London's bohemia – a place for the modern-day Bloomsbury set, where engineers now jostle with advertising executives and questionable media companies. But the Sanderson hotel possibly heralded the end of this era, and as Candy and Candy move to re-brand us as Noho and take Fitzrovia upmarket, we all become restless. Change is in the air, as Crossrail is about to be unleashed on us and the sorting office in Rathbone Place probably redeveloped – though at least that will spare us the mad afternoon rush of red vans.

Today we swim from point to point to avoid the family that seems to have laid claim to our beach – but perhaps they are the next generation of Pipers.

Mark Whitby is chairman of engineer Ramboll Whitbybird

Kathryn Firth...
outlines plans to revive Covent Garden

As London's oldest public square Covent Garden Piazza, with its market, has great civic and commercial importance. Over the centuries it has undergone many physical transformations though it has never ceased to be both public room and marketplace. Today Covent Garden is clearly on the 'tourist map' but it holds little appeal for Londoners or visitors seeking a more sophisticated experience. Congested and often disappointing, it is fulfilling neither of its roles as well as it could.

KPF is the masterplanner on a team Covent Garden London has assembled to revive Covent Garden. The aim is to retain its positive physical and social attributes while making changes that ensure it is one of London's – indeed the nation's – foremost public spaces and retail/cultural destinations. The biggest challenge is to find a balance between appreciating Covent Garden's heritage and differentiating it from the high street to become a vital urban centre. Covent Garden is far more diverse today than when it was a food market.

The masterplan aims to make the whole Covent Garden area more legible and permeable, with improvements to the public realm and some building redevelopment. Covent Garden must read as distinctive yet integrate well with other West End areas such as Chinatown, Soho and Seven Dials. While Covent Garden's heritage gives the area a unique character it should not be the only thing that defines it in the future.

The public realm must act as a stage supporting diverse events. Currently there is a tension between vast flows of people moving through the Piazza and adjacent streets, and the desire to stop, rest and watch. The seats in St Paul's Churchyard offer a rare moment of repose; more such opportunities must be provided. There should also be more choice in terms of movement, allowing people to discover courts and passages off the principal thoroughfares.

Not every part of Covent Garden need be all things to all people – but this incredible piece of London should offer something for everyone.

Kathryn Firth is senior associate principal with Kohn Pedersen Fox Associates

Terry Farrell...

summarises his new ideas for Bloomsbury

Bloomsbury's great squares are world-renowned as exemplars of urban planning. But what is their role today? The character of the surrounding area has changed so much, being almost entirely residential at first and now a mix of academia, museums, hotels and office premises. We want to preserve Bloomsbury's character as a green oasis in the West End but give each square a clear identity as part of an integrated landscape network.

A fundamental part of the plan is to create a new university 'high street'. Focused on Malet Street, the route will provide a new address for the numerous world famous institutions along its length, and also make strong links to the British Museum. Our initial ideas are to connect Wilkins' fine main quad of University College (pictured right) to Malet Place and create a series of linked 'quadrangles', which will allow the universities to work as a campus rather than a number of separate buildings. This strategy will also provide a new public setting for the northern entrance of the British Museum, linking Bedford Square to the west and Russell Square to the east.

Reducing the negative impact of through-traffic on Bloomsbury is vital. All the one-way roads must be converted to two-way, including the removal of the Tottenham Court Road and Gower Street gyratory. This will transform Gower Street, making it a local road once more.

How will this happen in practice? When it comes to masterplanning, I like to distinguish between an overarching vision and its related framework strategies – its detailed implementation through 'mini-masterplans'. The latter need enterprise and determination to carry out – the important thing is to continually refer back to the vision and the unifying leadership it provides.

Sir Terry Farrell is principal of architect and urban designer Farrells

Rosemary Ashton...
recalls a time of cultural and social innovation

When you mention Bloomsbury, most people think of Virginia Woolf and her 'set' of writers and artists living there in the early 1900s. But what was Bloomsbury like before it lent its name to the 'Bloomsbury Group'? In 1800 it was largely undeveloped, full of cesspits; by 1900 it was the hub of London's intellectual and cultural life.

Francis Russell, fifth Duke of Bedford, Bloomsbury's biggest landowner, decided in 1800 to develop his land. He and his successors employed the architects James Burton and Thomas Cubitt to build the fine squares and streets we still enjoy today.

The Russells were reforming politicians, and sold or lent their land for progressive educational institutions, the first being University College London, built in Neo-Classical style in 1826-8 by William Wilkins. Founded to offer university education to those unable to graduate from Oxbridge because they were not confessing Anglicans, it taught new subjects like modern languages and geography. University College Hospital was at the forefront of medical innovation, pioneering the use of anaesthetics in the 1840s.

From this beginning sprang other progressive institutions: closely connected with University College was the Ladies' College, founded in Bedford Square in 1849 to offer higher education to women. In the same year University Hall – now the Dr Williams's Library – was built in Gordon Square by Thomas Donaldson, professor of architecture at University College, as a hall of residence for students. Almost next door there rose in 1854 the most ambitious new church of the period, John Raphael Brandon's imposing Gothic structure, the Catholic Apostolic Church – now the University Church of Christ the King.

The last of Bloomsbury's 19th-century architectural and institutional highlights is perhaps the most interesting. Custom-built in Tavistock Place in 1897 by two young Bloomsbury-bred architects, A Dunbar Smith and Cecil Brewer, was the Passmore Edwards Settlement – now Mary Ward House (pictured left). Passmore Edwards, an uneducated self-made newspaper magnate, donated the money for this hall to organise play and learning sessions for Bloomsbury's poor children; in 1898 it opened the first school for disabled children in Britain. Architecturally significant both aesthetically and in its fitness for its intended use, it is a fine example of the best of Bloomsbury.

Rosemary Ashton is Quain Professor of English Language and Literature at University College London and the author of critical biographies of Samuel Taylor Coleridge, George Eliot, and Thomas and Jane Carlyle

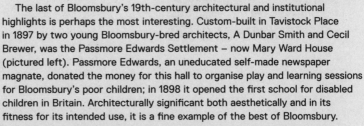

Roger Madelin...

explains the thinking behind the redevelopment of King's Cross

The previous plans for King's Cross were all too early. The 'railway lands' could only ever be ready for development when the railways were sorted. The final go-ahead to complete the transport infrastructure at King's Cross was only made after London won the 2012 Olympics. Without clarity of what the site is, or is to become, no proposal can be serious. 'What if?' options can be built in, but over-optimism is a disease of any 'boom' period. There will always be economic cycles.

The late 1980s plan which assumed that the Channel Tunnel link would arrive under central London from the south, with the new station being beneath the area between King's Cross and St Pancras, was fundamentally flawed. Were we all misguided or just blinded by the 1980s boom?

Offices are where most people in London work. Without office workers, there'd be no-one around to shop, eat or go to the theatre. But different types of offices or work spaces are needed to accommodate the diverse range of businesses that any successful city contains. Diversity is the key.

'People go where people are.' Offices alone don't make for a vibrant city. We must learn from successful existing places, with their streets of shops and restaurants, their residential neighbourhoods, their schools with diverse catchments, and their parks and external spaces.

The development area at King's Cross makes it the most significant opportunity in central London for over 150 years. London needed a say, for this development is London's – not just Argent's, or Camden's, or Islington's. There are big wins for all.

But Camden's lead, with the then Mayor's policies providing a wider perspective, has been essential. Debate about development should always be open to all but it must be well-informed and holistic. We have tried hard to encourage the widest debate with the facts – and this will continue.

Roger Madelin is joint chief executive of developer Argent

Jonathan Sergison...

examines the use of brick in Bloomsbury

London is a chaotic, complex, rich urban environment to work in and react against, and it continues to profoundly influence the way our practice thinks about architecture. The city is built in a clay valley and brick evolved as the most expedient material for realising both monumental, civic architecture and more lowly, ordinary structures.

The strict puritanical architecture of Georgian London is one that we often cite in our discussions. It is a language devoid of unnecessary embellishment externally (the interiors are a different matter). You realise you are in a largely Protestant country when you see how this building type evolved. Bloomsbury is one of the most planned parts of London, developed through the employment of 'pattern books' of standard house types. This results in an overall sense of urban wholeness, where repetition is the main feature.

Closer inspection reveals subtle variation because whole streets were rarely built by one developer builder and tended to grow in a more piecemeal manner. But the reading of brick as an individual element is suppressed in favour of an overall reading of a city block. The surface of the brick would be soot-washed to advance and anticipate the process of weathering that would naturally take place in the polluted London air. The brick used would be a London stock brick, which is ochre in colour, and the process of soot-washing creates a much more abstract and powerful building language.

In his building for the British Medical Association (pictured left), Edwin Lutyens explored a plastic language in his handling of brickwork. It was rubbed and cut in a manner normally reserved for stonework. The result is a highly modelled facade that understands the need for an exaggeration of detail in the typically soft London light. The principal elevation refers to the earlier domestic architecture of Georgian Bloomsbury, but Lutyens was fully aware of the civic purpose of this building. The brick he chose is smaller than usual in its vertical dimension, subliminally emphasising the building's height and grandeur.

An ambiguous role is played by brickwork in some 1950s buildings for London University. The facade of the Birkbeck College library is more glass than brick, and the glazing assemblies are brought close to the surface to mask the structural members at the window head. Like many other educational buildings in Bloomsbury, this building reads as a large-scale revised version of the domestic architecture built a hundred years before.

All these examples punctuate my journey to and from work. They are like old friends to me, as I have been observing them for 20 years, first as a student and then as an architect. I am reminded in this of the objects, mostly bottles, collected by Giorgio Morandi. His lifetime work was their study, rearrangement and rendition as still life paintings. Similarly, through careful observation, London reveals enough material to inform our entire architectural production.

Jonathan Sergison is a partner in Sergison Bates Architects. There are more observations on the area in 'Sergison Bates Architects: Papers 2' (2007)

Simon Bradley...

hails the restoration of St Pancras Station

St Pancras Station (1867-77) is surely the most improbable of all London's great buildings. Its physical form is startling enough: Sir William Barlow's mighty single-span train shed, and the red brick Gothic towers and spires of Sir George Gilbert Scott's Midland Grand Hotel at the station frontage. But if the Midland Railway had achieved its intended merger with the rival line at Euston, the company would not have needed a terminus here at all. Had Barlow then chosen to tunnel the Midland's new line under the Regent's Canal (as at King's Cross next door), rather than crossing it by viaduct, the great arched train shed would never have soared so high.

And what if the competition to design the hotel had been handled more fairly? After all, Scott entered only by special request, and the rules on cost limits had to be bent to let him win. The railway then ran so short of money that the hotel had to be erected in two phases. The full design, with its quadrant wing and great staircase on the British Library side, came close to being abandoned altogether.

The very survival of St Pancras is lucky too. Conversion of the hotel to offices in the 1930s saved the interiors from modernisation. Demolition plans in the 1960s were fought off (Euston was not so lucky). A perfectly serious proposal in the 1990s to dig a giant hole for a new Eurostar terminus between St Pancras and King's Cross was dropped in time. Instead, the magnificently restored St Pancras is now the portal to the Continent. The conversion has been drastic in some ways, but also imaginative and inspiring. The hotel is being restored too. London can be proud of both.

Simon Bradley is editor of the Pevsner Architectural Guides (Yale University Press) and author of St Pancras Station (Profile Books, 2007)

Gillian Darley...
explores the magical Soane Museum

No architect ever contrived such a monument to himself as John Soane. Puncturing the still relatively self-effacing north side of Lincoln's Inn Fields is a sudden assertive explosion of stonework. Designed to salute the irresistible rise of its architect occupant, 13 Lincoln's Inn Fields was a deliberate eye-catcher. No wonder the authorities gave Soane a difficult ride.

The challenging, even unsettling, atmosphere intensifies on entering the house that Soane entrusted to the nation in 1833, by Act of Parliament. Over the years and throughout Soane's continual refinements and alterations, it became the summation of his idiosyncratic architecture. His handling of the ground plan creates an intense spatial complexity. From the moment of leaving the reassuringly familiar entrance hall and adjoining dining room-cum-library, it becomes increasingly impossible to disinter the three storeys of the two-and-a-half conjoined terraced houses, so brilliantly have they been elided, their interlocking forms explored as verticals, horizontals, ellipses and more.

Every inch of the house-museum refers to Soane's work elsewhere. Tiny passages and exquisite links echo his great lost masterpiece, the Bank of England, while the golden Breakfast Parlour (*pictured below*) with its tissue-thin hanging canopy, and Soane's very particular vocabulary of ornament, is a miniaturised, doll's house version of many of his great rooms elsewhere. Here the walls and ceiling of a modest room have been peeled away, sliced into, lifted up and reassembled, so that natural light can pour in, leaving reflection, refraction and shadow to carry on the dancing visual enchantment. It is, quite simply, the most wonderful little room in London.

The other unifying thread in this literally fabulous house is the fact that 13 Lincoln's Inn Fields is an autobiography. Every object here has some resonance, some link with Soane's life. It was this three-dimensional revelation, a cabinet of curiosities of a uniquely personal order, that prompted me to embark on a biography of the man – much of it researched in the first-floor library at 12 Lincoln's Inn Fields, the Soanes' first family house.

Gillian Darley is the author of biographies of John Soane and John Evelyn

Maps

This is a very selective guide to the architecture
of a large central area of London. Arranged
chronologically, it spotlights individual buildings
but also streets and squares. For a fuller history
of how particular properties or sites have evolved,
readers should consult the relevant volumes in
Nikolaus Pevsner's Buildings of England series,
which list almost everything of architectural interest

01
King's Cross

To the north of St Pancras and King's Cross stations is the 67 acre site of Argent's King's Cross development. Immediately east is the Regent Quarter, with old industrial buildings adapted to new uses and new insertions at a similar scale. Further east is the Priory Green Estate, one of several post-war social housing schemes by Berthold Lubetkin (architect of the Highpoint flats in Highgate in the late 1930s).

The Euston Road is a real barrier, severing this area from Bloomsbury to the south. It's no pleasure to walk along, but once you're past the British Library, with its inviting courtyard, you can continue on quieter streets. Somers Town, which extends northwards, is defined by social housing. Particularly worth a look is the LCC's Ossulston Estate, which echoes Viennese schemes of the 1920s.

There's no trace now of the demolished Euston Arch, whose site was swallowed up by the rebuilt Euston Station, which is now set to be redeveloped by Foreign Office Architects and Allies and Morrison. West of the station, Drummond Street and Euston Street retain a late-Georgian character. Then comes another major development that is still in progress: Regent's Place. Walking west past this down Longford Street brings you to one of the key sites in this book – St Andrew's Place, where Denys Lasdun's Royal College of Physicians and John Nash's Neo-Classical terrace sit harmoniously side-by-side.

02
Bloomsbury

A landmark on the southern edge of Bloomsbury is Nicholas Hawksmoor's St George's Church, recently restored and with an excellent interior. A meandering walk north from here can include the Georgian set-piece, Bedford Square, as well as the plainer, more formulaic architecture of Bedford Place or Gower Street, while Torrington Square gives the best sense of how the university precinct has evolved.

UCL's commitment to medicine is evident in a cluster of buildings between Gower Street and Tottenham Court Road, which introduce an abrupt change of scale – found also when you emerge from intimate Woburn Walk, with its Georgian shopfronts, and see Lutyens' attempt at grandeur with his British Medical Association on Tavistock Square.

In much of Bloomsbury there's a tension between the domestic and the monumental – and not just when the university or British Museum is involved. Look at the flamboyant Hotel Russell on Russell Square; its architect built a similarly grand hotel nearby, demolished in the 1960s. Just east of the Russell is the ambitious Brunswick Centre, revitalised after some troubled years. Domesticity returns in the terraces of Doughty Street, John Street and Great James Street – while a walk east beyond the edge of Bloomsbury (and edge of the map) shows it continuing in the Lloyd Baker Estate and neighbouring squares.

03
Covent Garden

Many visitors to Covent Garden probably think of it as just the market hall and nearby streets, not the large area slated for redevelopment in the 1960s. Perhaps the market itself looks best from the fifth-floor terrace of the Royal Opera House, created in the renovation by Dixon Jones. Apart from Inigo Jones' St Paul's Church, none of the buildings around the square date from its foundation; the most prestigious survivor is 43 King Street, but lurid salmon stucco conceals its brickwork.

Walking south-west takes you to part-pedestrianised Trafalgar Square with its galleries and Gibbs' St Martin-in-the-Fields – a model for many churches around the world. But if you head north up Endell Street you see the polychrome brickwork of E M Barry's National School building, while in Langley Street old warehouses loom above you. Leaving the market behind brings the character of this area into focus and shows what the 1960s conservationists were trying to save. You could wander here for ages before finding Goodwin's Court, with its row of late-18th century shopfronts.

Almost as unobtrusive is the Phoenix Community Garden on Stacey Street – an ideal place to escape the crowds. It's in the parish of St Giles, which was once notorious for crime and poverty. Perhaps Renzo Piano's Central Saint Giles will turn its fortunes around, but only if it creates a genuine *place*, not a replica of countless others.

04
Holborn

The Inns of Court may appear to be private but on weekdays they're open to all. With its successive buildings of different styles and periods, Lincoln's Inn is a perfect example of a place that has grown in an accretive way, with each new element adding to the overall richness. Nikolaus Pevsner declared of Gray's Inn: 'It is English visual planning at its best.'

If the Inns of Court can seem exclusive, so too until recently did one of London's grandest 18th-century buildings, William Chambers' Somerset House. It is now a cultural centre, with a spectacular staircase (the Navy Stair) and a restaurant that spills out onto a terrace overlooking the Thames. Quite close by is Street's Royal Courts of Justice: an intricate complex with a long Gothic hall at its heart. The Lloyds Bank across the street used to be the courts' restaurant – hence its piscine decorations in blue-grey majolica.

Sandwiched between the Royal Courts and Lincoln's Inn Fields is the London School of Economics, which has several new additions. Lincoln's Inn Fields was one of the first sites in the city's westward expansion, developed at the same time as Covent Garden's Piazza, and a building here (Lindsey House) is attributed to the Piazza's architect, Inigo Jones. On the square's north side, where the 18th, 19th and 20th centuries are all in evidence, is an attraction no visitor should miss – Sir John Soane's Museum.

05
Soho

Soho's former fields can still be traced in its pattern of streets and alleys. Golden Square was the earliest development but the architectural mix is richer in Soho Square. Adapted Georgian buildings rub shoulders with Victorian and 20th century ones, while afternoon sun illuminates the red brick of St Patrick's, its stock-brick Georgian neighbour, and Centre Point beyond.

Albeit altered or dishevelled, some pockets of attractive Georgian architecture survive: Dean Street is a good hunting ground, as too are Meard Street and Broadwick Street – the latter also containing Richard Rogers' Ingeni. Elsewhere the 20th century has left its mark in such contrasting sights as the timbered atrium of Liberty's department store – an Olde English fantasy – and the suave Jazz Age Deco of Raymond Hood's Ideal House.

John Nash's 'triumphal way' marks the western edge of Soho in the form of Regent Street, currently being regenerated by the Crown Estate. It continues south to Waterloo Place where it is flanked on either side by splendid Regency clubs – the United Service, the Athenaeum – while the backdrop is one of London's first high-rise offices, RMJM's New Zealand House. When you stand at the top of the steps by the Duke of York's Column you are poised between two distinct worlds: the built-up central zone of London to the north, the parks and Westminster unfolding to the south.

06
Fitzrovia

It's no surprise to find a book called *Characters of Fitzrovia* (Pimlico, 2002). For years the area has proved hospitable to a wide range of trades, professions and people (both dissolute and distinguished). The architecture has helped. Only Fitzroy Square has had aspirations to grandeur but it wasn't in fashion for long. The more modest Georgian buildings have been easy to adapt (accommodating offices, restaurants and galleries) and still give a strong identity to parts of the area: Percy Street, for instance, or the charming little enclave of Colville Place.

But while 'good ordinary' buildings like these gain lustre by simply surviving, nothing is so precious here that interlopers can't be tolerated: among them, William Butterfield's forceful All Saints, Margaret Street; the vaguely Art Nouveau flats in Candover Street by H Fuller Clark; the YMCA near Fitzroy Square by Festival of Britain designer Ralph Tubbs; and the full-blooded Brutalism of Lyons, Israel & Ellis' PCL building.

On the west of Fitzrovia is Nash's 'triumphal way', which incorporated the Adam brothers' Portland Place in its route. Although much modified, it is still recognisable; the blatant intruders being Broadcasting House and the Langham Hotel, whose bulk makes Nash's elegant All Souls Church more toy-like than it is. Just one street west of here is Robert Adam's Chandos House – a model of refinement and restraint.

King's Cross

01

01 **St Pancras Old Church.**
    12th cent onwards (with garden
    that includes the Soane Family
    Tomb by *John Soane*, 1816)

02 **Drummond St, Euston St.** c.1820

03 **Park Square.** *John Nash,* 1823-5

04 **Holy Trinity.** *John Soane*, 1826-8

05 **Keystone Crescent.** c.1845

06 **King's Cross Station.**
    Lewis Cubitt, 1851-2;
    currently being renovated by
    John McAslan + Partners

07 **German Gymnasium.**
    E A Gruning, 1864-5

08 **Stanley Buildings.** 1864-5

09 **St Pancras Station and Midland
    Grand Hotel.** *George Gilbert Scott,
    W H Barlow,* 1868-74;
    station restored and extended
    by *Pascall & Watson* and
    Rail Link Engineering, 2004-7

10 **Euston Station lodges.**
    J B Stansby, 1869-70

11 **Albion Yard and neighbouring
    Regent Quarter blocks.**
    Late 19th cent; redeveloped by
    RHWL Architects, 2004 onwards

12 **6, St Chad's Place.**
    Late 19th cent; remodelled by
    Squire and Partners, 2004

13 **Regent's Wharf.**
    1890s onwards; redeveloped by
    Rock Townsend, 1991

14 **Fire Station.**
    LCC Fire Brigade Branch, 1901-2

15 **Porters South and North,**
    Crinan St. Early 1900s; remodelled by
    Fitch Benoy, 1988, and *DEGW,* 1989

16 **London Edinburgh and Glasgow
    Assurance building.**
    Arthur Beresford Pite, 1907

17 **Ossulston Estate (Chamberlain
    House, Levita House)**
    G Topham Forrest (LCC), 1927-31

18 **195 North Gower St.**
    Maxwell Fry, 1939-40

19 **Priory Green Estate.**
    Skinner, Bailey & Lubetkin,
    1947-57; *Avanti Architects,* 2000

20 **Royal College of Physicians.**
    Denys Lasdun, 1961-4

21 **Oakshott Court.**
    Camden Architect's Dept, 1972-6

22 **British Library.**
    Colin St John Wilson, 1978-97

23 **Speech, Language and Hearing
    Centre,** St Christopher's Place.
    Troughton McAslan, 1995

24 **Regent's Place.**
    *Arup Associates, Sheppard Robson,
    Farrells, Wilkinson Eyre,* 1998 onwards

25 **Squire and Partners' office,**
    77 Wicklow St.
    Squire and Partners, 2002

26 **Gagosian Gallery,** 6-24 Britannia St.
    Caruso St John, 2003-4

27 **Kings Place,** York Way.
    Dixon Jones, 2008

28 **KX200.**
    Allford Hall Monaghan Morris, 2008

29 **King's Cross (Argent)**
    Under construction

Bloomsbury

02

01 **St George the Martyr,**
Queen Square. 1705 onwards;
remodelled by *S S Teulon*, 1867

02 **St George,** Bloomsbury Way.
Nicholas Hawksmoor, 1716-31;
restored by *Molyneux Kerr*
with *Inskip + Jenkins*, 2006

03 **St George's Gardens.**
Early 18th century burial ground,
now garden

04 **Great Ormond St.** c.1721

05 **Great James St.** 1720s

06 **5 and 5a Bloomsbury Square.**
Henry Flitcroft, 1744

07 **John St.** 1756-9

08 **Bedford Square.** 1775-86
(No 1 by *Thomas Leverton*)

09 **Gower St.** 1780s onwards

10 **Doughty St.** 1792-1820

11 **Bedford Place.**
James Burton, 1801-5

12 **Cartwright Gardens.**
James Burton, 1807

13 **Mecklenburgh Square.**
Joseph Kay, c.1808 onwards

14 **St Pancras New Church.**
H W & W Inwood, 1819-22

15 **Gordon Square.**
Thomas Cubitt, 1820s onwards

16 **Woburn Walk.**
Thomas Cubitt, c.1822

17 **British Museum.** *Robert Smirke*,
1823-52; Round Reading Room
by *Sydney Smirke*, 1854-7;
King Edward VII Wing by *John
Burnet*, 1906-14; Great Court by
Foster and Partners, 1994-2000

18 **University College.**
William Wilkins, 1827-9

19 **Regent Square.**
One side remaining from c.1829

20 **Argyle Square.** c.1840-49

21 **Christ the King.**
Raphael Brandon, 1853

22 **Mary Ward House.**
A D Smith and Cecil Brewer, 1895-7

23 **Russell Hotel.**
C Fitzroy Doll, 1898

24 **University College Hospital.**
Alfred and Paul Waterhouse,
1896-1906; *Llewellyn Davies
Yeang*, 2005

25 **British Medical Association.**
Edwin Lutyens, 1911-25

26 **Heal's.** *A Dunbar Smith
and Cecil Brewer*, 1912-17

27 **30 Russell Square.**
John Burnet, 1913-14

28 **New London Architecture,
Building Centre (former
Daimler showrooms).** c.1920

29 **Victoria House.** *Charles W Long*,
1921-34; *Alsop Architects*, 2003

30 **London School of Hygiene
and Tropical Medicine.**
P M Horder and V O Rees, 1926-8

31 **Former YWCA,** Great Russell St.
Edwin Lutyens, 1930-2

32 **Former Daimler garage,
now offices,** Herbrand St.
Wallis, Gilbert & Partners, 1931

33 **Senate House and Library.**
Charles Holden, 1932-7

34 **SOAS.** *Charles Holden*, 1940;
library by *Denys Lasdun*, 1968-73

35 **Congress House.**
David du R Aberdeen, 1953-7

36 **Library,** Theobalds Rd.
Sidney Cook (Holborn Borough
Architect), 1960

37 **Brunswick Centre.** *Patrick
Hodgkinson*, 1968-72; *Hodgkinson*
with *Levitt Bernstein*, 2006

38 **Bloomsbury Theatre.**
Fello Atkinson, 1964-9

39 **Institute of Advanced
Legal Studies and Institute
of Education.**
Denys Lasdun, 1965-76

40 **Dept of Chemistry.** *Architect's
Co-Partnership*, 1969

41 **19-29 Alfred Place.**
Richard Seifert & Partners, c.1972

42 **German Lutheran Church,**
Sandwich St.
Maguire & Murray, 1974-9

43 **Stewart House.** *Shepheard,
Epstein & Hunter*, 1985

44 **Imagination,** 25 Store St.
Remodelled by *Herron Associates*,
1988-9

45 **Housing block,** Little Russell St.
Avanti Architects, 1988-91

46 **ITN,** 200 Gray's Inn Rd.
Foster and Partners, 1989-92

47 **29 Endsleigh Gardens.**
Avanti Architects, 1992-4

48 **Brunei Gallery and SOAS
Extension.**
Nicholas Hare Architects, 1995

49 **Clore Management Centre,**
Torrington Square.
Stanton Williams, 1996-7

50 **RADA extension.**
Avery Associates, 2000

51 **The Place,** 16 Flaxman Terrace.
Allies and Morrison, 2001

52 **Birkbeck College extension,**
Torrington Square.
Nick Evans Architects, 2004

53 **School of Slavonic and East
European Studies,** Taviton St.
Short and Associates, 2005

54 **Gibbs Building, Wellcome Trust.**
Michael Hopkins & Partners, 2005

55 **Torrington Square**
Robert Myers Associates, 2006

56 **Centre for Nanotechnology,**
7-19 Gordon St.
Feilden Clegg Bradley, 2006

57 **UCL Cancer Institute.**
Grimshaw, 2007

58 **Roberts Building,** Torrington
Place. *Grimshaw*, 2008

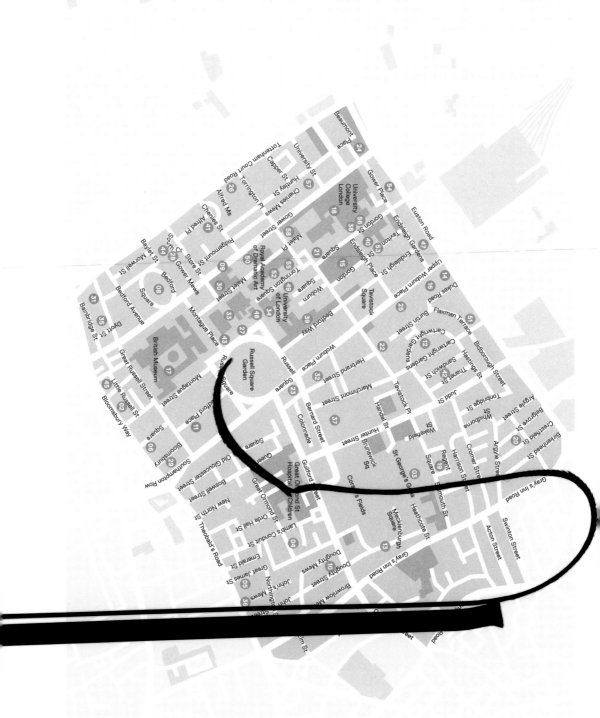

Covent Garden

03

01 **York Water Gate.** 1626-7

02 **Covent Garden:** Piazza, 1629-37;
Market House by *Charles Fowler*,
1828-30; Flower Market
(now London Transport Museum)
by *W Cubitt & Co*, 1871-87,
and *Avery Associates*, 2007

03 **St Paul Covent Garden.**
Inigo Jones, 1631-5

04 **Buckingham St.** 1675 onwards

05 **King St.** Early 18th century
onwards (No 43 probably
by *Thomas Archer*, 1717)

06 **St Martin-in-the-Fields.**
James Gibbs, 1721-6;
Eric Parry Architects, 2008

07 **Craven St.** 1730s onwards

08 **St Giles-in-the-Fields.**
Henry Flitcroft, 1731-3

09 **Southampton Place.**
Henry Flitcroft, 1757-63

10 **Royal Society of Arts,**
John Adam St. *Robert and
James Adam*, 1772-4

11 **6-10 Adam St.** *Robert and
James Adam*, early 1770s

12 **Goodwin's Court.** Late-18th century

13 **Theatre Royal,** Drury Lane.
Benjamin Dean Wyatt, 1810-12

14 **St Martin's National School,**
Adelaide St.
George Ledwell Taylor, 1830

15 **Royal Opera House.** *E M Barry*,
1857-8; *Dixon Jones and BDP*, 1997-9

16 **Langley St / Shelton St.**
Mid-19th century warehouses

17 **22 Endell St.** *Withers*, 1859

18 **St Giles National Schools,**
Endell St. *E M Barry*, 1860

19 **Garrick Club,** Garrick St.
Frederick Marrable, 1864

20 **James Smith's umbrella shop,**
53 New Oxford St. c.1870

21 **Princess Louise,** 208 High Holborn.
Late 19th century

22 **The Salisbury,**
90 St Martin's Lane. 1898

23 **Coliseum.** *Frank Matcham*, 1902-4

24 **Country Life building,**
8 Tavistock St.
Edwin Lutyens, 1904-5

25 **Sicilian Avenue.** *R J Worley*, 1905-10

26 **Zimbabwe House.**
Charles Holden, 1907-8

27 **Westminster County Court.**
H N Hawkes, 1908-9

28 **Holy Trinity,** Kingsway.
Belcher & Joass, 1909-11

29 **Kodak House,** 65 Kingsway.
John Burnet, 1911

30 **Freemasons Hall.**
Ashley & Newman, 1927-33

31 **Centre Point.**
Richard Seifert & Partners, 1959-66

32 **St Martin's Lane Hotel.**
Richard Seifert & Partners,
1964-6; *Harper Mackay*
and *Philippe Starck*, 1999

33 **Space House.**
Richard Seifert & Partners, 1964-8

34 **Odhams Walk.**
Donald Ball (GLC), 1974-81

35 **Comyn Ching Triangle.**
Adapted/restored by *Farrell
Grimshaw Partnership*, 1978-85

36 **Phoenix Community Garden.**
1980s onwards

37 **Embankment Place.**
Terry Farrell & Co, 1986-91

38 **Hungerford Bridge.**
Lifschutz Davidson and
WSP Group Engineers, 2002

39 **8-9 Long Acre.**
Kohn Pedersen Fox, 2004

40 **Bridge,** Floral St.
Wilkinson Eyre, 2004

41 **City Lit,** Keeley St.
Allies and Morrison, 2005

42 **Central St Giles.** Under construction:
Renzo Piano Building Workshop

St Giles

Royal Opera House

Covent Garden & Market

Seven Dials

Charing Cross

Station

N

Holborn

04

01 **Lincoln's Inn,** including
Old Buildings, c.1490-1520; Chapel,
1619-23; New Square, 1680-1690s;
Stone Buildings by *Robert Taylor*,
1774-80; New Hall and Library by
Philip Hardwick, 1842-5

02 **Gray's Inn,** including Hall,
1556-8; Chapel, 16th cent
onwards; the Walks, early 17th
century; courtyards from late
17th and 18th century; 10 South
Square by *Raymond Erith*, 1970-2

03 **Staple Inn Buildings,**
High Holborn. 1580s

04 **Lindsey House,**
59-60 Lincoln's Inn Fields.
Attributed to *Inigo Jones*, 1639-41

05 **St Clement Danes.**
Christopher Wren, 1668-82

06 **Essex St.** 1675 onwards

07 **Newcastle House.**
William Winde, 1685-9

08 **St Mary-Le-Strand.**
James Gibbs, 1714-17

09 **Bedford Row.** Early 18th century

10 **57-58 Lincoln's Inn Fields.**
Henry Joynes, 1730

11 **Somerset House.** *William
Chambers*, 1776-1801; *Inskip +
Jenkins*, 1998-2000; *Donald Insall
Assocs* and *Dixon Jones*, 2000

12 **Sir John Soane's Museum,**
12-14 Lincoln's Inn Fields.
John Soane, 1792-1837

13 **King's College.**
Robert Smirke, 1829-31; chapel
by *George Gilbert Scott*, 1861-4

14 **Royal College of Surgeons.**
Charles Barry, 1835-6; Hunterian
Museum remodelled by *Julian
Bicknell & Associates*, 2005

15 **Royal Courts of Justice.**
George Edmund Street, 1871-2

16 **Prudential Assurance.**
Alfred Waterhouse, 1876-1901

17 **Lloyds Bank,** 222-225 Strand.
Goymour Cuthbert and
W Wimble, 1882-3

18 **Former branch of Bank of
England (now a pub),** 194 Fleet St.
Arthur Blomfield, 1886-8

19 **40-42 Kingsway.**
Edwin Lutyens, 1906

20 **99 Aldwych.** *John Burnet*, 1909-11

21 **44-46 Kingsway.**
Metcalfe & Grieg, 1914-15

22 **Bush House.**
Helmle & Corbett, 1920-8

23 **Summit House.**
Westwood & Emberton, 1925

24 **India House.**
Herbert Baker, 1928-30

25 **LSE,** Portugal St. Library by
Foster and Partners, 1999-2001;
John Watkins Plaza by *MacCormac
Jamieson Prichard*, 2003

26 **Great Turnstile House.**
Mary Thum Associates, 2006

27 **LSE,** 24 Kingsway. Grimshaw, 2008

28 **Silken Hotel.** Under construction:
Foster and Partners

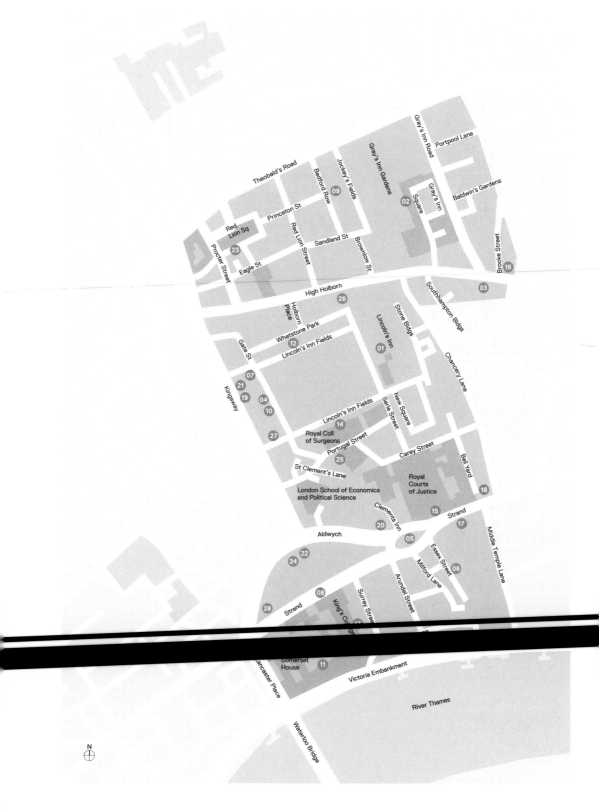

Gray's Inn Road
Portpool Lane
Theobald's Road
Bedford Row
Jockey's Fields
Gray's Inn Gardens
09
Gray's Inn
Square
02
Baldwin's Gardens
Princeton St
Red
Lion Sq
Red Lion Street
Sandland St
Brownlow St
Brooke Street
16
Procter Street
23
Eagle St
High Holborn
Southhampton Bldgs
03
26
Holborn
Place
Stone Bldgs
Lincoln's Inn
Whetstone Park
12
Lincoln's Inn Fields
Gate St.
01
Chancery Lane
07
21
19 **04**
10
Kingsway
Lincoln's Inn Fields
Serle Street
New Square
14
Royal Coll
of Surgeons
27
Portugal Street
Carey Street
Bell Yard
25
St Clement's Lane
London School of Economics
and Political Science
Royal
Courts
of Justice
18
Clements Inn
15
Strand
Aldwych
20
17
05
22
Essex Street
24
Milford Lane
06
Middle Temple Lane
08
Arundel Street
28
Strand
King's Co
Surrey Stree
Somerset
House
11
Victoria Embankment
Lancaster Place
River Thames
Waterloo Bridge

N

Soho

05

01 **Golden Square.** 1675 onwards
    (now largely 20th century)

02 **Soho Square.** 1677 onwards

03 **6-7 Frith St.** 1718

04 **48-58 Broadwick St.** 1722-3

05 **Meard St.** 1722-33

06 **Dean St.** 1730s houses
    (no 88 is a 1791 shopfront)

07 **House of St Barnabas,**
    1 Greek St. 1744-6

08 **Our Lady of the Assumption,**
    Warwick St.
    Joseph Bonomi, 1789-90

09 **St Anne Soho.** Tower
    by *S P Cockerell, 1801-3*

10 **Royal Opera Arcade.**
    John Nash and G S Repton, 1816-18

11 **Theatre Royal,** Haymarket.
    John Nash, 1820-1

12 **Suffolk Street.**
    Renewed by *John Nash, 1820-4*

13 **United Service Club.**
    John Nash, 1826-8

14 **Athenaeum.**
    Decimus Burton, 1827-30

15 **Carlton House Terrace.**
    John Nash, 1827-33

16 **Duke of York's Column.**
    B D Wyatt, 1831-4

17 **National Gallery.**
    William Wilkins, 1833-8;
    Venturi, Rauch & Scott Brown,
    1987-91; Dixon Jones, 2004

18 **Trafalgar Square.** 1830s onwards;
    Foster and Partners, 2003

19 **Palace Theatre.** *G H Holloway*
    and T E Colcutt, 1888-91

20 **National Portrait Gallery.**
    Ewan Christian and J K Colling,
    1890-5; Dixon Jones, 1998-2000

21 **French Protestant Church,**
    Soho Square. *Aston Webb, 1891-3*

22 **St Patrick,** Soho Square.
    John Kelly, 1891-3

23 **Novello's (now Chappell),**
    160 Wardour St.
    Frank L Pearson, 1906-10

24 **Burberry's,** 18-22 Haymarket.
    Walter Cave, 1911-13

25 **Liberty's,** Great Marlborough St.
    E T and E S Hall, 1922-3

26 **Regent Street Quadrant**
    Reginald Blomfield, 1923-8

27 **Piccadilly Circus underground**
    station. *Charles Holden, 1925-8*

28 **Ideal House,**
    Great Marlborough St.
    Raymond Hood, 1927-9

29 **Lex Garage,** Brewer St.
    J J Joass and Robert Sharp, 1928-9

30 **Notre Dame de France,**
    Leicester Place.
    H O Corfiato, 1951-5

31 **New Zealand House.**
    Robert Matthew, Johnson-Marshall
    & Partners, 1957-63

32 **Soho Lofts,** 90 Wardour St.
    Conversion by *CZWG, 1995*

33 **Bourchier St.** Flats by *Koski,*
    Solomon & Ruthven, 1995-8

34 **Ingeni,** 17 Broadwick St.
    Richard Rogers Partnership,
    1998-2000

35 **Soho Theatre,** 21 Dean St.
    Paxton Locher, 2000

Oxford Street

Oxford
Circus

Ramillies Pl

Gt Chapel St

Hollen St

21   Soho

Sutton Row

22   Goslett Yard

Carlisle St

Square   07

Noel Street

23

02

Manette St

Poland Street

Richmond Mews

03

Dean Street

35

Greek St

Argyll St

28

Great Marlborough Street

Berwick Street

Wardour Street

Frith St

25
Little
Marlborough
St

Marshall Street

04

34

Hopkins St

Broadwick Street

05   Meard St

06   Old Compton Street

Romilly Street

19

Carnaby Street

Lexington Street

Peter St

33

Bourchier St

Regent Street

Kingly Street

Gt Pulteney St

32

09

Shaftesbury Avenue

Newport Pl

Charing Cross Road

Beak Street

29

Rupert Street

Gerrard Street

Golden
01
Sq

Bridle Lane

Brewer Street

Great Windmill Street

Lisle Street

30   Cranbourn St

Warwick St

08

Sherwood St

Denman St

Coventry St

Whitcomb Street

Leicester St

Leicester
Square

Glasshouse St

Irving St

Regent Street

26

27

Piccadilly Circus

St Martin's St

20

St Martin's Place

St Albans St

Panton St

Orange St

17

Regent Street

Haymarket

24

11   12   Suffolk St

18   Trafalgar Square

Charles II St

31

Pall Mall East

10

Cockspur St

Carlton House Terrace

16

N

Fitzrovia

06

01 **Percy St.** 1764-7

02 **Colville Place.** 1760s

03 **Chandos House.**
Robert Adam, 1769-71

04 **Chandos House stables.**
Robert Adam, 1769-71;
Arthur Bolton, 1924

05 **Fitzroy Square.**
Robert Adam, 1793-8

06 **Park Crescent.**
John Nash, 1812-22

07 **All Souls,** Langham Place.
John Nash, 1822-4

08 **All Saints,** Margaret St.
William Butterfield, 1849-59

09 **Langham Hotel.** *Giles & Murray,*
1863; *Halpern Partnership,* 1990

10 **All Saints Church House
and School.** *William Butterfield,* 1870

11 **Rising Sun,** 46 Tottenham
Court Rd. *Treadwell & Martin,* 1896

12 **York House, Tower House
and Belmont House,** Candover St.
H Fuller Clark, 1903

13 **All Souls School,** Foley St.
Arthur Beresford Pite, 1906-8

14 **21 Little Portland St.**
Arthur Beresford Pite, c.1910

15 **34-38 Mortimer St.**
F L Pither & F M Elgood, 1915

16 **General Medical Council,**
44 Hallam St. *Eustace Frere,* 1915-22

17 **Broadcasting House.**
G Val Myers, 1931; *MacCormac
Jamieson Prichard,* 2002 onwards

18 **19-23 Wells St.**
Richardson & Gill, 1931

19 **Royal Institute of British
Architects.** *Grey Wornum,* 1932-4

20 **YMCA Indian Student Hostel.**
Ralph Tubbs, 1952

21 **Sanderson,** Berners St.
Slater, Moberly Uren, 1957-64;
Philippe Starck, 2000

22 **British Telecom Tower.**
*Ministry of Public Building
and Works,* 1964

23 **Polytechnic of Central London
School of Engineering & Science
(now University of Westminster).**
Lyons, Israel & Ellis, 1965-8

24 **Arup's offices,** 13 Fitzroy St.
Sheppard Robson, 2004

25 **Noho Square
(Middlesex Hospital site).**
Under construction: *Make*

Regent's Park

Park Square
Gardens

Regent's Park

06

Park Crescent

Cresent Mews

Bridgeford Mews

Bolsover Street

Greenwell
Street

Portland Place

19

Portland Place

Hallam Street

Great Portland Street

Carburton Street

Cleveland Street

Clipstone Mews

Clipstone Street

Euston Road

Warren Street

Conway St.

Fitzroy Sq.

Fitzroy
Mews

St Luke's
Hospital

05

Conway St.

Grafton Mews

Maple St.

Fitzroy Street

Maple Pl.

Cypress Place

20

Cleveland
Mews

22

Charlotte St.

24

Whitfield St.

Charlotte
Mews

Tottenham Court Road

University
College
London

Tottenham
Mews

Tottenham St.

Scala St.

Whitfield St.

Howland Street

23

Ogle St.

13

Goodge Pl.

Goodge Street

02

11

New Cavendish Street

Mansfield St.

04

03

Duchess Street

17

07

Langham Street

Langham Pl.

Chandos St.

09

Great Titchfield Street

Gosfield St.

Hanson Street

Foley Street

12

Riding House Street

Nassau St.

25

Mortimer Street

Berners Mews

Rathbone St.

Windmill Street

01

Percy Street

Percy Ms

Stephen Ms

Stephen St.

Gresse St.

University of
Westminster

15

Little
Titchfield St

Wells Street

Wells Mews

18

21

Berners Street

Newman Pass

Newman Street

Rathbone Place

Henway Pl

Henway Street

University of
Westminster

Little Portland Street

14

Margaret Street

08

10

Marylebone
Passage

Eastcastle Street

Berners Place

Gt Castle St

Market Pl

Winsley St.

Oxford Street

N

There are many people that NLA would like to thank for making this publication possible.
Special thanks to Andrew Mead for his expertise and invaluable editorial direction. Sarah Douglas and Lee Belcher at Wallpaper* Magazine require special mention for their time, enthusiasm and dedication to this project. Thanks also to Catherine Slessor and Dominik Gigler for their significant contributions, Dominic Bell for his cartography, Isabel Allen for her comments and suggestions, Kate Groves for picture research and Bill Young for proofing and fact-checking.

NLA would like to thank the following for their help in providing information and images on projects featured: Rumi Kubukawa, Manhattan Loft Corporation; Alison Stawarz, John McAslan + Partners; Richard Thompson, Dixon Jones; Sharon Nolan, Make; Jo Cutts, Foster and Partners; Jeremy Castle, Legal and General; Emma Davies, Farrells; John Futcher, London Borough of Camden; Anna Strongman, Argent; Julie Stuber, Crossrail and Jon Fawcett, The British Library.

We would like to give special thanks to our Principal Sponsors for their ongoing support of NLA: Argent, Argyll, City of London, Ramboll Whitbybird and The Building Centre.

This book was published on the occasion of the London Festival of Architecture 2008 and was inspired by the commitment and energy of all those involved in the King's Cross, Bloomsbury, Fitzrovia and Covent Garden Hub. Thank you to Peter Murray, Sarah Ichioka and the LFA08 team for their support.

Special thanks are due to Hub Chair, President and Provost Professor Malcolm Grant, University College London, and the advisory group: Sir Terry Farrrell, Farrells; Helen Gordon, Legal & General; Neil MacGregor, British Museum; Piers Masterson, London Borough of Camden; John Hennessy, Abbey; David Partridge, Argent; Brett Steele, Architectural Association; John Turzynski, Arup and Mark Whitby, Ramboll Whitbybird.

Thanks are also extended to the Bloomsbury Improvement Group for their advice and support: Jim Murray, Bloomsbury Project Management; Mark de Rivaz, The Bedford Estates; Simon Neale, City of Westminster; Bryn Morris, The Institute of Education; Claire O'Connor, London School of Hygiene and Tropical Medicine; Sharon Page, SOAS; Colin Henderson, The Building Centre; Kevin Flynn, University College London Hospital; Suzanne Spooner, University of London; Philomena Gibbons, The Wellcome Trust and Peter Bishop, Design for London.

The delivery of our Hub programme would not have been possible without our Hub Sponsors: CABE, Derwent London and the London Borough of Camden and our Co-Sponsors: Ramboll Whitbybird; The Building Centre; Price & Myers; University College London; The Wellcome Trust; Capita, Corus and The Bedford Estates. The help of our partner organisations is also gratefully acknowledged and we extend thanks to The British Museum, Somerset House and Targetfollow.

NLA would like to thank everyone who played a part in the transformation of Montague Place: Richard Howey, Steeldeck; William Whitby, Arup; Piers Roberts, Designersblock; Jack Tilbury, Charcoal Blue; Bob West, John Futcher and Robert Slaney, London Borough of Camden; Philippa Edwards, Joanna Mackle, Joe Edwards, John Orna-Ornstein and Susan Raikes, The British Museum; Nigel Thorne, Landscape Institute and Ian Lanchbury, Student Landscape Institute Council. Kevin Carmody, Andy Groarke and Berit Bessell of Carmody Groake require a special mention for their dedication and tireless work, without which the NLA Sky Walk would not have been possible.

Finally, a big thank you to all the individuals and organisations who have contributed an event, venue or their enthusiasm to the success of the King's Cross, Bloomsbury, Fitzrovia and Covent Garden Hub. It has been a pleasure to work with you all.

FRANCIS FRITH'S
TOWN & CITY
MEMORIES

CHRISTCHURCH

MICHAEL A HODGES MA, FCIPD, MCMI, has been a regular soldier, Officer of Customs and Excise, management consultant and personnel manager. Michael was Mayor of Christchurch Borough 1978/9 and a councillor for eleven years while commuting daily to London. He is life member and former Chairman of: Christchurch Local History Society; Friends of Red House Museum; Society of Ley Hunters; a former Chairman of Dorset Earth Mysteries Group; and life member of Christchurch Conservation Trust; New Forest Association and Friends of Christchurch Priory. He is author of local histories: *Prepared for Battle; The Smuggler No Gentlemen; The Ghosts of Christchurch Hundred; Christchurch Castle; Christchurch the Golden Years; Christchurch Monographs.*

CHRISTCHURCH, WICK FERRY, WEST LANDING 1900 45045

FRANCIS FRITH'S

TOWN&CITY

MEMORIES

CHRISTCHURCH

MICHAEL A HODGES

FRANCIS FRITH'S
TOWN & CITY
MEMORIES

First published as Christchurch, A Photographic History of your Town in 2001 by
Black Horse Books

Revised edition published in the United Kingdom in 2005 by
Frith Book Company Ltd as Christchurch, Town and City Memories.

Limited Hardback Edition 2005
ISBN 1-84589-004-3
Paperback Edition 2005
ISBN 1-85937-956-7

British Library Cataloguing in Publication Data

Christchurch
Town and City Memories
Michael A Hodges

Frith Book Company Ltd
Frith's Barn, Teffont,
Salisbury, Wiltshire SP3 5QP
Tel: +44 (0) 1722 716 376
Email: info@francisfrith.co.uk
www.francisfrith.co.uk

Aerial photographs reproduced under licence from Simmons Aerofilms Limited
Historical Ordnance Survey maps reproduced under licence from Homecheck.co.uk

Printed and bound in England

Front Cover: **CHRISTCHURCH, CHURCH STREET 1900** 45053t
The colour-tinting in this image is for illustrative purposes only,
and is not intended to be historically accurate

FRANCIS FRITH'S
TOWN & CITY
MEMORIES

CONTENTS

The Making of an Archive	6
Christchurch from the Air	8
Introduction	10
Prehistory	12
Saxon Burgh	16
The Normans	26
The Manors	34
The Priory	42
County Map	52
The Civil War	54
Smuggling	56
Brabner's Map	68
Victorian Times	70
The Twentieth Century	76
Ordnance Survey Map	84
Names of Pre-Publication Buyers	86
Index	87
VOUCHER FOR FREE MOUNTED PRINT	91

THE MAKING OF AN ARCHIVE

F rancis Frith, Victorian founder of the world-famous photographic archive, was a devout Quaker and a highly successful Victorian businessman. By 1860 he was already a multi-millionaire, having established and sold a wholesale grocery business in Liverpool. He had also made a series of pioneering photographic journeys to the Nile region. The images he returned with were the talk of London. An eminent modern historian has likened their impact on the population of the time to that on our own generation of the first photographs taken on the surface of the moon.

Frith had a passion for landscape, and was as equally inspired by the countryside of Britain as he was by the desert regions of the Nile. He resolved to set out on a new career and to use his skills with a camera. He established a business in Reigate as a specialist publisher of topographical photographs.

Frith lived in an era of immense and sometimes violent change. For the poor in the early part of Victoria's reign work was a drudge and the hours long, and ordinary people had precious little free time. Most had not travelled far beyond the boundaries of their own town or village. Mass tourism was in its infancy during the 1860s, but during the next decade the railway network and the establishment of Bank Holidays and half-Saturdays gradually made it possible for the working man and his family to enjoy holidays and to see a little more of the world. With characteristic business acumen, Francis Frith foresaw that these new tourists would enjoy having souvenirs to commemorate their days out. He began selling photo-souvenirs of seaside resorts and beauty spots, which the Victorian public pasted into treasured family albums.

Frith's aim was to photograph every town and village in Britain. For the next thirty years he travelled the country by train and by pony and trap, producing fine photographs of seaside resorts and beauty spots that were keenly bought by millions of Victorians.

THE RISE OF FRITH & CO

Each photograph was taken with tourism in mind, the small team of Frith photographers concentrating on busy shopping streets, beaches, seafronts, picturesque lanes and villages. They also photographed buildings: the Victorian and Edwardian eras were times of huge building activity, and town halls, libraries, post offices, schools and technical colleges were springing up all over the country. They were invariably celebrated by a proud Victorian public, and photo souvenirs – visual records – published by F Frith & Co were sold in their hundreds of thousands. In addition, many new commercial buildings such as hotels, inns and pubs were photographed, often because their owners specifically commissioned Frith postcards or prints of them for re-sale or for publicity purposes.

In order to gain some understanding of the scale of Frith's business one only has to look at the catalogue issued by Frith & Co in 1886: it runs to some 670 pages. By 1890 Frith had created the greatest specialist photographic publishing company in the world, with over 2,000 stockists! The picture on the right shows the Frith & Co display board on the wall of the stockist at Ingleton in the Yorkshire Dales (left of window). Beautifully constructed with a mahogany frame and gilt inserts, it displayed a dozen scenes.

POSTCARD BONANZA

The ever-popular holiday postcard we know today took many years to appear, and F Frith & Co was in the vanguard of its development. Postcards became a hugely popular means of communication and sold in their millions. Frith's company took full advantage of this boom and soon became the major publisher of photographic view postcards.

Francis Frith died in 1898 at his villa in Cannes, his great project still growing. His sons Eustace and Cyril continued their father's monumental task, expanding the number of views offered to the public and recording more and more places in Britain, as the coasts and countryside were opened up to mass travel. The archive Frith

created continued in business for another seventy years. By 1970 it contained over a third of a million pictures of 7,000 cities, towns and villages. The massive photographic record Frith has left to us stands as a living monument to a special and very remarkable man.

This book shows your town as it was photographed by this world-famous archive at various periods in its development over the past 150 years. Every photograph was taken for a specific commercial purpose, which explains why the selection may not show every aspect of the town landscape. However, the photographs, compiled from one of the world's most celebrated archives, provide an important and absorbing record of your town.

CHRISTCHURCH FROM THE AIR 1934   AFR280

INTRODUCTION

Christchurch, a town, a parish, and a municipal and parliamentary borough in Hants. The town stands on the peninsula at the confluence of the rivers Avon and Stour, with a station on the L. & S.W.R., 98 miles from London, 10 NW by W of the Needles, and 21 SW by W of Southampton. It possibly was founded by the ancient British, or more probably by the Romans, and it has yielded traces of a Roman temple to Mars. It was known to the Saxons as **Tweonea** or **Tweoxnea**, and it is mentioned in the Saxon Chronicle in connection with the contest for the crown in **901** between Edward the Elder and his kinsman Ethelwald. The manor of it belonged at Domesday to the Crown, and bore then the name of Thuinam or Twineham, and it was given by Henry I. to Richard de Redvers, and passed to the Montacutes and the Nevilles. A monastery was founded at it by King Athelstan, rebuilt as a collegiate church by Flambard, the architect of Durham cathedral, and converted into an Augustinian priory in 1150 by Baldwin de Redvers, and this occasioned the name to be changed into Christchurch, at first Christchurch-Twineham. Town walls and a castle were erected by either Richard or Baldwin de Redvers.

The description of the town given in Brabner's Gazetteer of 1895 (see left) is now known to contain errors. There is no Roman temple dedicated to Mars, although Christchurch Priory may well be on the site of a Roman building. The Saxon name of Christchurch was Tweoxneam (the place betwixt the waters), it was a burgh: a fort, built on the orders of Alfred the Great, against the Vikings. The original Saxon Minster was probably founded in the 7th century, around the time of St Birinus or St Aldhelm. Brabner's description of the

HURN ROAD, AT THE BLACKWATER FERRY 1900
45047

The modern Hurn Road passes over the Wessex Way motorway close to this point. The picture shows the east bank of the Stour at Blackwater. This road was used by smugglers' wagons. Today it links Christchurch to the Airport.

Priory Church was too early to mention The Royal British Legion Chapel of Remembrance, at the west end of the south aisle of the nave. The motte and bailey castle was built in the late 11th century; the stone constable's hall was added in the middle of the 12th century, and the stone keep late in the following century. St Catherine's Hill, north of the town, has many Bronze Age barrows but no watchtowers, although it was the site of a Roman signal station and Tudor and Napoleonic invasion beacons. Hengistbury Head is now part of Bournemouth, a suburb of Christchurch until 1855. The borough has an area of 12,776 acres and includes the parishes of Hurn and Burton, and the village of Highcliffe. It has a population of 45,000 people. Christchurch was transferred to Dorset in 1974. The Borough Council has 24 members and there are five county councillors; the local MP represents Christchurch and East Dorset. Christchurch is the oldest borough in Dorset still with a Royal Charter, allowing a mayor to chair the council.

THE BLACKWATER FERRY ON THE RIVER STOUR 1900
45048

To reach Holdenhurst, the Stour was crossed just north of Bosley three miles from Christchurch. The crossing was by a punt using a cable. The Stour was also crossed by: a ferry at Wick to reach Hengistbury; an iron toll bridge, of the 19th century, at Tuckton; a 13th century stone bridge at Iford to reach Bournemouth, closed to traffic when a modern bridge was built in the 1920s.

PREHISTORY

Neolithic farmers may have used St Catherine's Hill and the site of Christchurch Priory for rituals, perhaps involving sun worship; various alignments (ley lines) pass through both these places.

About 4,000 years ago, when the climate became wetter and sky gods were subject to competition from water gods, the confluence of the rivers Avon and Stour may have been used for religious rituals. Some folklore may relate to this, such as the story of the dispute as to where the church should be built.

St Catherine's Hill was initially chosen and the stones transported there, but every morning the stones had been miraculously moved to the confluence, where the church was therefore built. This story may be a memory of conflict between Neolithic and Bronze Age religions, long before Christianity.

During the Bronze and Iron Ages, the main settlement in the area was the promontory fort at Hengistbury Head, linked to Christchurch by ferry. It is possible that Phoenician traders came to Hengistbury for Mendip lead and silver, in exchange for wine and jewellery. Caesar's conquest of Gaul, about 45 BC, interrupted the foreign trade, which never recovered. The Roman invasion in AD 43, by the 2nd Augusta Legion, captured the hill forts of Wessex.

A scattering of Roman and British artefacts in Christchurch town has been concentrated in the area of the monastery and along the road from the Priory towards Wimborne. There was clearly a high status Roman building in Christchurch, perhaps under the Priory. Pagan religious activity was known on the monastery site: a cist of bird bones was found in 1765.

The Roman invaders had substantial initial resistance from the local Durotrigians, and later faced attacks from seaborne raiders, so they built a chain of coastal forts. The signal station on top of St Catherine's Hill would have linked Corfe and Carisbrooke, which may have been Roman forts. In AD 285 Britain was taken over by a usurper emperor: the Romans re-invaded through the Solent in AD 296, but in AD 383 another usurper denuded Britain of troops, leaving it open to raiders. Perhaps for these reasons Hengistbury Head was finally abandoned for Christchurch, which was more easily defended from the sea: coin hoards of the time have been found in the area.

Arthur, the Roman British war leader, probably regarded the Avon as a boundary between the Britons and the Saxons.

WICK FERRY, WEST
LANDING 1900
45045

Bicycling was clearly
popular. The young
woman is a picture in
her ankle length skirt,
long sleeved blouse and
straw boater. The boat
on the left is a fishing
punt of the type known
as a Marsh Tub, once
used for carrying tubs
of smuggled spirits over
shallows where customs
keel boats could not
follow. The boat in the
centre is a Marsh Punt
of the type used for wild
fowling, the large calibre
punt gun required the
punt be aimed rather
than the gun.

ABOVE:
THE PRIORY CHURCH AND MONASTERY WALL FROM THE
RIVER STOUR 1900 45042

The monastery wall still survives. Smugglers frequented this area for
centuries.

RIGHT:
THE RIVER STOUR 1918 68054

This view shows a wide variety of sailing dinghies and, a ketch rigged
ship's lifeboat conversion, a salmon punt, a wildfowler's marsh punt,
a gaff rig sailing dinghy, two small cutters, two motor fishing boats
or ferries.

RIGHT:
CHRISTCHURCH FROM
WICK 1903 49163

There is a sailing barge
lying at Clay Pool at the
confluence of Avon and
Stour. Such barges carried
coal to Christchurch Quay.

CENTRE :
WICK FERRY, WEST BANK 1900 45044

The Ferry punt is ready to cross the Stour with the ferryman and two

RIGHT :
WICK FERRY, EAST LANDING c1955 C99158

The Ferry is still a punt, but with a motor and a dozen passengers.

THE PRIORY CHURCH AND CHRISTCHURCH QUAY, FROM WICK 1918 68053

The old Sailing Club with its verandah is on the right. The club was founded in 1883 and the clubhouse opened in 1896. It moved to a new building in the 1960s.

P agan Saxons settled on the gravel spur, which became Christchurch. It has been suggested that Cerdic and Cynric (a Saxon father with a Celtic-named son), who landed at Cerdic's Ora, and were the first sea-borne Saxon settlers in Hampshire, actually landed at Christchurch Harbour.

It is likely that Christchurch Priory was built at a place of pre-Christian religious activity. The pagan cemetery was at Bargates. The Saxons at Tweoxneam were probably converted to Christianity in the early 7th century.

Attacks by Viking pirates caused King Alfred to create burghs, so that no one was more than 20 miles from a place of refuge. The defences at Tweoxneam (later known as Twynham) required 470 warriors to man the wall. Each warrior was supported by one hide of land which provided for him and his family; hence not all lived inside the town. Later a group of one hundred hides became one administrative area. By 1316, the hundred ran from the (now old) county boundary with Dorset, along the coast and incorporated Lymington and Bournemouth, although the latter was then the unoccupied Liberty of Westover (the River Stour).

The area's defences made use of the rivers Avon and Stour, the marshes, the Mill Stream and the walls of the monastery. Thus, as in 1940, only the neck of the promontory needed a wall. The corner of the iron stone-faced wall can be seen at Druitt Gardens and Bank Close.

Christchurch Quay (see 86275, p.18) was used to import goods such as slate, stone and coal, and export timber, grain and beer. The mast and yard (seen on the left of the picture) and the shelter on the quay no longer exist.

The Mill Stream (C99231, p.21), merging with the Stour beyond the swans, separates Place Mill and the old sailing clubhouse. In the early 20th century the mill was used as a boathouse but still retained its milling machinery. It has now been restored and is open to the public.

C99208, p.22), was a Saxon site recorded in the Domesday Book. It has been used both to grind corn and full cloth: a process involving shrinking and beating, or pressing, the yarn to make cloth heavier and more compact. It is unique - a freshwater tide mill linking two main rivers.

Saxon Burgh

ABOVE :
SWANS ON THE RIVER STOUR C1955 C99200

Mute swans breed as a pair for life. This scene is off Quomps, land
that was originally marsh.

BELOW :
CHRISTCHURCH QUAY 1934 86275

THE PRIORY CHURCH AND THE BANDSTAND FROM QUOMPS c1955 C99228

The bandstand is a 1930's addition. At the time of this picture, there is also a crazy golf course on the left. Ices, teas and café advertisements are all more visible.

Saxon Burgh

CHRISTCHURCH QUAY c1955 C99078

Teas are being advertised on the old tearoom roof (the building has since been replaced). There are now more boats on the river available for hire.

FEEDING THE SWANS AT CHRISTCHURCH QUAY c1955 C99231

CONVENT WALK AND THE RIVER AVON c1955 C99082

Convent Walk was laid out in 1911 for the Coronation of George V.

SAXON BURGH

PLACE MILL AND
CHRISTCHURCH
QUAY c1960
C99208

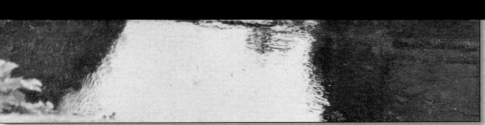

Saxon Burgh

Convent Walk, River Avon, the Mill Stream and Castle Garde-Robe c1955   C99109

The Mill Stream water level needed to be controlled at the mill pool: to power the mill and for defence, and also to flush the garde-robe (toilet). Hengistbury Head is visible on the horizon on the right, beyond the river. A Dutch barge is moored in the Avon.

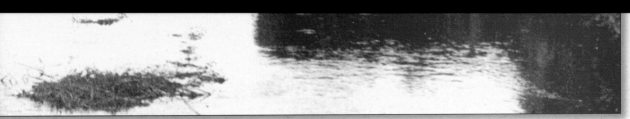

THE NORMANS

THE PRIORY CHURCH AND THE RIVER AVON FROM THE TOWN BRIDGE 1906 55904

This summer picture shows weed in the river; beyond is the Mill Stream parallel with the Avon. The 12th-century Constable's Hall is overgrown with ivy.

THE NORMANS

The Norman Conquest brought new overlords and a motte and bailey castle was built in the town. Besides guarding the harbour and access inland, Christchurch Castle also protected Sarum from attack from the sea. However, the Minster occupied the highest land in the town and the builders of the castle had to respect the church having the prime site.

About 1079 the Forest Laws, introduced by William II, created the New Forest - situated roughly between the Avon and Southampton Water. The New Forest was unpopular; it dispossessed people and others lost their livelihood. History has blamed Sir Walter Tirrel for the murder of William II, but on his deathbed he denied involvement. However, the church had financial reasons for wanting the King out of the way and it has been suggested that Ranulph Flambard, the Bishop of Durham and a former Dean of Christchurch, was the murderer. It was Flambard who promoted the rebuilding and substantial enlargement of the Church. It is likely that parts of the earlier Saxon Minster survive in the crypts of the Priory church.

Christchurch is listed in the Domesday Book of 1086 as 'part of the Hundred of Edgegate', meaning 'Gate at the Edge of the New Forest'. Domesday states that Twynham had a value of £19, reduced to £10 following the conquest, plus: 'What is in the Forest assessed at £12.10 shillings'. Domesday lists the lands held by the Canons of Holy Trinity, Twynham: 'Value before 1066 £6; now £8'. The church of Holy Trinity Twynham – later Christchurch – owned land in other places outside the Forest.

In 1100, Henry I granted the castle to his cousin, Richard de Redvers. Richard's son, Baldwin, lost Christchurch during 'The Anarchy' in 1136; his possessions were later restored. In 1147, Walter de Pinkney seized Christchurch Castle. De Pinkney brutally mistreated his prisoners and the townsfolk; as a result he was battleaxed to death in the churchyard.

his possessions. He was Lord of the Manor, and granted the town its first Charter. The present Royal Charter, dated 1974, is the most recent of a long line. The Charter granted the burgesses, on behalf of the townspeople, certain tolls of the market. The market place was at the junction of High and Castle Streets, and expanded down the High Street towards the bargate. Christchurch Monday Market

THE NORMANS

CHRISTCHURCH
CASTLE BAILEY, THE
BOWLING GREEN AND
CONSTABLE'S HALL
C1955 C99108

In this view the ivy has been
cleared from the hall. The
damaged building was used
as a stone quarry in the
18th century, until the vicar
prevented the vandalism. The
height of the green above
the ground level of the hall
indicates how much the level
has been raised.

continued until 1871; it was restarted in 1976 in Bank Close, but has now returned to the High Street. In time, besides the market, there were two fairs, each of three days. These were at Trinity on 19 June and St Faith's Eve on 17 October - they were abolished in 1872.

In 1149, Baldwin also introduced 26 Augustinian monks to the Priory; Augustinians were cheap since they worked to support themselves. Setting up a monastery gained influence with the Church, which was the civil service of the time, as well as gaining merit for the Hereafter. The married lay canons were evicted from the Priory and the celibate Austins took over. They continued the rebuilding of the Priory church and the monastery, probably at about the same time Baldwin built the constable's hall, next to the Mill Stream at the northeast corner of the bailey. The building was of considerable luxury for the time; it had mullion windows and a fireplace with a cylindrical chimney (one of only five in England). A garde-robe was built in about 1210, and a watergate about 1240.

The keep was built three storeys high with nine-foot-thick walls, perhaps after 1293, when the castle passed to William de Montacute, later Earl of Salisbury. The plan of the building is oblong, with splayed angles at the corners as a defence against mining. The castle at Christchurch was featured in Conan Doyle's novel, 'The White Company', which places its action around 1365.

CHRISTCHURCH CASTLE, CONSTABLE'S HALL AND KEEP, FROM THE SOUTHEAST 1900 45051

The keep is built on the original Norman motte, the hall was for the use of the resident Constable of the Castle and, in its day, was the height of luxury.

CHRISTCHURCH CASTLE BAILEY, THE BOWLING GREEN AND MOTTE, WITH RUINS OF THE KEEP C1955 C99099

The roofs of houses can be seen on the site of the castle ditch. The motte had its level raised to create platforms for artillery in the Civil War.

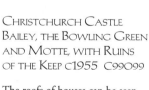

THE NORMANS

CHRISTCHURCH CASTLE, CONSTABLE'S HALL AND KEEP 1900 45050

The Castle saw action in 'The Anarchy', before the hall was built, and later in the Civil War. The ground floor of the hall is looped, for use by bows. Since Norman times, several English kings have visited the castle. It would be feasible to restore the hall, with an oak roof and first floor.

THE MANORS

The person who held the castle held the manor, which was governed by the Manorial Court; this would have been held in the hall. Later the Court House was a building in Castle Street, often wrongly believed to be what is now the New Forest Perfumery. The Prior was lord of a church manor.

The Malmesbury family now holds the manor of the borough and the Meyrick family holds the manor of Christchurch, which includes the castle keep. The church land, governed by the Prior, was confiscated in 1539, hence the Priory manor ceased to exist.

In 1336 the Hundred Years War began, which saw many French raids on the coast. During the war the citizens of Salisbury built a man-of-war: 'The Trout', which was taken down the Avon for fitting out at Christchurch. The troubled times may have prompted the construction of the bargate, which was removed in 1724. However, it gave its name to the road 'Bargates' which continues the High Street north to the railway.

In 1455, the Civil Wars - known as the Wars of the Roses - began. The castle was held for the Duke of Salisbury and Warwick, at a rent of one red rose a year. He was killed in 1471 and Christchurch passed to the Duke of Clarence. Clarence was murdered in The Tower in 1478, drowned in a butt of malmsey. Christchurch was then held for a white rose until the victory of Henry VII.

A lazar house (a hospital for infectious diseases) dedicated to St Mary Magdalen, was set up before 1317, during a period when diseases were being brought into the country by returning crusaders. The Priory, and its monastery, provided medical care for townsfolk and a hostel for visitors - as well as the care of souls. The education that was available was generally for servants of the church; services were in Latin, and the bible was not available in the vernacular. Hence, all was in the hands of priestly interpretation, often by an ill-educated clergy.

Churches were places full of colour: the Priory was painted inside so that the aisle ceilings represented blue skies with stars, and the piers blazed with vivid colours. The laity were taught through stories, pictures and even sculptures. Churches could carry pagan symbols like the Green Man - there is one in the Priory. There are also carvings on the misericords and bench ends inside the quire, some of which have pagan associations. One such is a carving known as 'the Wild Man', which shows a nude male figure with a club in his right

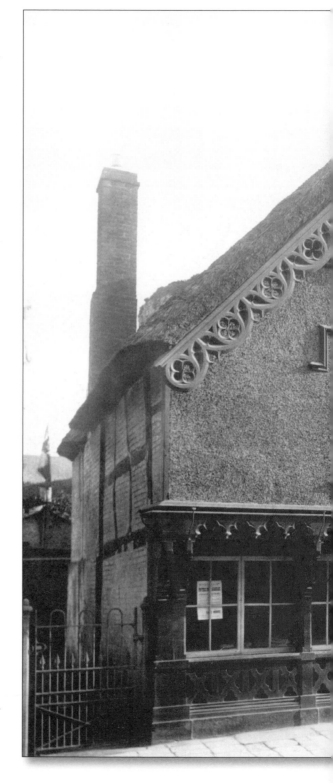

THE MANORS

This is now the New Forest Perfumery. It is perhaps the oldest council house in England and has often been miscalled 'the old court house'. However the court-leet (a kind of manorial court that some lords were entitled to hold) met in a building on the left of the house. The courthouse was dismantled in 1884.

hand, like the Cerne Giant. In the left hand is a shield with a face upon it; the Cerne Giant used to have a cloak over his left arm and a severed head in his left hand, so there are further similarities.

The Priory became well known for its relics of the murdered Archbishop of Canterbury, Thomas á Becket: the illiterate people of the time were credulous, as were most of the clergy. However, the monks at Christchurch were able to come up with an unusual relic, the Miraculous Beam, which can still be seen. This was a beam for the construction of the nave: to the dismay of the builders it was found to be too short; however, the following morning it had miraculously been lengthened and fitted perfectly. The monks also told the tale of the silent carpenter who worked on the church, yet never appeared for his wages.

The Priory had its own seal that showed it once had a central tower, which fell in the 12th century. The borough also has its own seal, made in the Rhineland in about 1330, and still available for use.

The borough has two maces, the oldest dating from 1616. The other mace was made in 1969, at Christchurch Barracks - then operated by Royal Engineers. The maces are carried in front of the mayor on ceremonial occasions. They symbolise royal power, hence in the presence of the Monarch, or the Lord Lieutenant of the County, they are carried reversed.

A vital part of the medieval economy, aspects of which still exist, was the right to the use of commons. These rights are attached

CASTLE STREET,
FROM OPPOSITE
THE KINGS ARMS,
LOOKING TOWARDS
THE HIGH STREET
C1955 C99084

The King's Arms Hotel, on the right, was rebuilt in 1803. It has since been known as Humby's Commercial Hotel, and Newlyn's Family Hotel. The market and town hall once stood at the end of Castle Street, at the junction with High Street. The building on the right, at the High Street end, is Lloyds Bank. It is on the site of the former Wilts and Dorset Bank, which was once the White Hart Inn.

to land, not to individuals, although the occupier of the land exercises the rights for his own use. There were many commons in Christchurch. Some still exist such as Cowherd's Marsh, which is controlled by the Commoners Association.

Commons used to operate through the medieval court leet, which ░░ an account of the past year, income and expenditure. Complaints were heard and, if required, fines levied. Officials for the coming year were appointed, including: a bailiff (to collect revenues); constables and tithing men (to keep law and order); a hayward (also town crier), who managed the commons and the pound for strayed animals; a breadweigher (weights and measures) and an aletaster.

The aletaster had to check the price and quantity of ale, and also test its strength. He did this by visiting a beer house whenever it had a new brew: the landlord had to exhibit a green branch outside as a sign. Some ale was poured onto a wooden seat and the aletaster, wearing leather breeches, sat in the puddle for 20 minutes or so, ░░ no good. This is because sugar made the leather stick to the wood under the warmth and pressure of the aletaster's body - strong ale did not stick. Christchurch still has a volunteer aletaster and a volunteer town crier.

ABOVE:
THE MILL STREAM, TOWN BRIDGE AND THE RIVER AVON C1955 C99232

The Mill Stream not only supplied the energy for the mills, it was also the eastern line of defence for the town. The north end of Convent Walk is shown between the Mill Stream and the Avon.

BELOW
THE TOWN BRIDGE AND RIVER AVON 1900 45049

Vessels travelling to and from Salisbury had to be narrow to pass through the piers of the bridge. Masts would be struck whilst passing beneath.

This photograph gives a view across the island, between the Avon and Little Avon. The first shop-front, on the left, was the 1914 Post Office and the second was the Christchurch Times office. The three-storey brick building next to it is 10 Bridge Street; in 1940 this was HQ of the local Home Guard, on the site of the house of the dishonest Supervisor of Riding officers, built in 1784. The building on the right is Bridge Place.

THE MANORS

THE PRIORY CHURCH FROM THE CASTLE
MOTTE 1906 55905

This photograph was taken from the south side of
the keep's Civil War artillery platform. The wall
at the front of the picture marks the castle ditch;
beyond is the garden of Church Hatch, which was
once the home of Hutchinson, the publisher.

THE PRIORY

One of the most important events in the history of Christchurch was the dissolution of the monasteries in 1539. As a result the monks had to leave, and the monastery and all its property was seized for Henry VIII, who gave the church to the town. The ownership of the church and its churchyard, was confirmed in the 18th century, when parishioners successfully prosecuted a vicar for keeping his cattle in their churchyard.

The Priory nave was commenced in 1094, and added to the west end of the earlier Saxon Minster. Several people have smelled frankincense in the nave. In the 1970s the author complained to the vicar about incense being used - this time the ghostly smell occurred in the area of the altar. The vicar replied that incense had last been used in 1539.

The transepts were built during the reign of Henry I, and the triforium in the reign of his grandson, Henry II. The nave roof was not completed until the 1190s and the story of the Miraculous Beam may date from this time; the aisles were vaulted about ten years later. In the Great Quire, the earliest misericord dates from 1210, the most recent from 1515. These misericords were small seats for monks to rest their buttocks on during services where they had to stand for long periods. The name misericord is taken from the knight's dagger, used to put a wounded victim out of his misery by administering the coup de grâce – the death stroke.

The north porch was started when Edward I's Queen was Lord of the Manor. This large porch was used as an early town hall. It was also used for weddings; the monastic church not wishing to involve its celibate monks in wedding ceremonies. About 1350 the Jesse Screen was carved in the Great Quire. There is a ghost story associated with the Great Quire: people working in the vestry, when the church was locked, heard heavy footsteps in the aisle. The footsteps sounded loud, like wooden pattens on a tiled floor – although the aisle was carpeted. On investigation, no one was found.

The Lady Chapel, at the east end of the church, was completed about 1390 and vaulted about 50 years later. In 1460, the tomb of Sir John and Lady Chideoke was installed. The west tower of the church, with its defensive characteristics, was built in the time of Edward IV, a monarch who was also a Lord of the Manor.

The last Prior of Christchurch was John Draper, elected in 1520. Draper was described as 'a conformable man' by Commissioners who

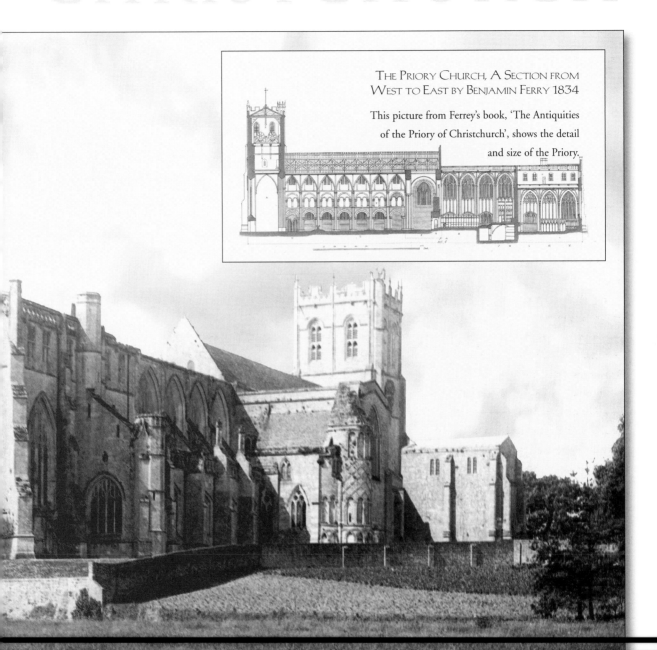

THE PRIORY CHURCH, A SECTION FROM
WEST TO EAST BY BENJAMIN FERRY 1834

This picture from Ferrey's book, 'The Antiquities
of the Priory of Christchurch', shows the detail
and size of the Priory.

THE PRIORY CHURCH FROM THE RIVER AVON 1890 25203

The Avon has been an important thoroughfare. The area in the right foreground below the Priory was once known as 'The Werkes' where stone from the Isles of Purbeck, and Wight, was taken for the castle and Priory. It is possible that stones from Wales were rafted up the Avon for Stonehenge.

THE PRIORY

THE PRIORY
CHURCH, THE NAVE
1918 68046

This Norman nave is
the longest of any parish
church; the Miraculous
Beam was originally in
the nave. The reredos is
shown hung with flags
of the victorious Allies.
Chairs have replaced the
19th-century pews.

THE PRIORY CHURCH, EAST END
OF NORTH FACE 1890 25207

The unfinished parapet on the roof
of St Michael's Loft (above the Lady
Chapel) dates from the dissolution of the
monasteries, when work was stopped.

visited the Priory. He appeared to co-operate with the dissolution and to surrender the Priory and its wealth. He was granted a huge pension, and given the Grange at Somerford to live in. He died in 1553 and was buried in the nave in front of the altar. His tombstone has been moved to lie in front of the Draper Chantry. There is no record of the silver gilt-plated statues, which stood in the niches of the Jesse Screen. These metal-covered carvings of saints, are thought by some to have been hidden by Draper in the church.

One of the Lords of the Manor was Margaret, Countess of Salisbury, and governess of Princess Mary – the daughter of Henry VIII. Henry's divorce caused the Church in England to split from Rome. However, Margaret remained faithful to the Roman Catholic Church; one of her sons became a priest in Rome and wrote a book calling for a united Church. She and her other two sons were arrested: one son was executed and the other exiled. The old countess was held in The Tower, where she was executed. She refused to kneel for the headsman and stood while an executioner's sword was used. The Pope appointed her son Cardinal Pole, Archbishop of Canterbury, in the reign of Queen Mary.

Above the Lady Chapel is St Michael's Loft, once the town's grammar school for boys: now a museum for the Priory. There are many interesting exhibits including part of a Saxon font, possibly of the original Minster. There are also ghost stories associated with the

THE PRIORY CHURCH, THE NORMAN THROUGH 1892

The north side of the nave is shown looking northwest. Remains of medieval wall paint exist: a reminder of a time when churches were ablaze with colour. The Priory still had pews in this photograph.

INSIDE THE NORTH PORCH 1918 68051

The north porch was used for meetings of 'The Sixteen', the Burgesses in the era before the town hall council.

loft. One story (a sworn affidavit is on show) refers to something pushing past a person on the spiral stairs leading to the loft, and a transparent figure standing in the doorway, then retreating and vanishing. Another, very recent event, was a case of automatic writing. A priory official, alone on duty in the museum, heard a crash above his head and then began to write in archaic French. When translated, the writing referred to an ex-Templar monk, Stephen, son of Richard de Montreuil, who was kept as a perpetual novice after the Order was disbanded. The night after his experience, the priory official had a dream in which he was informed that Stephen's mother was Angelique de Tournac. Also, the noise of a mason working has been heard in the Priory, when no work was in progress.

ABOVE;
THE ENTRANCE FROM THE
NORTH PORCH 1890 25210

The north porch was once used to store civic equipment, for example: the ducking stool for use in the Mill Stream, the whirly-gig used to make miscreants sick and giddy, and the Parish fire engine.

LEFT;
THE CHURCHYARD; THE ELM

Regrettably the Avenue no longer exists, due to the ravages of Dutch elm disease. Some famous visitors have walked the Avenue, including: Kaiser Bill (1907), and Queen Elizabeth II (1956).

THE PRIORY

THE PRIORY

THE SHELLEY MONUMENT 1918 68050

This monument to the poet, who drowned in Italy, is situated below the tower. It shows Mary Shelley, who wrote the Frankenstein's Monster story, lamenting over her husband.

THE NORTH
QUIRE AISLE
AND SALISBURY
CHANTRY 1890
25219

The Chideoke Tomb
is below the window.
Scrapings were taken
from it to mix with
water to seek to cure eye
problems. The beautiful
Salisbury Chantry
never held the body of
Margaret, Countess of
Salisbury.

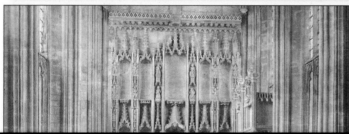

THE JESSE SCREEN AT THE GREAT QUIRE 1918
68048

This end of the quire is raised over the central crypt.
The Jesse Screen tells the story of the family tree of
Jesus. The empty niches would once have held wooden
statues covered with silver gilt.

THE PRIORY

ABOVE:
THE SOUTH FACE OF THE SALISBURY CHANTRY 1890 25217

This lovely chapel had its Salisbury Arms defaced by the Commissioners for the Dissolution of the Monasteries, to ingratiate themselves with Henry VIII.

RIGHT:
THE LADY CHAPEL 1918 68049

This most easterly part of the church lies below St Michael's Loft, which was once a boys' grammar school. There were many ghostly events here, and there are fine views over the harbour. The Lady Chapel has the flag of USAAF 405 Fighter Bomber Group from Christchurch Airfield, also the flag of the Christchurch Loyal Volunteer Artillery of the Napoleonic Wars.

THE MONTACUTE CHANTRY 1890 25221

The Montacute family were Lords of the Manor. The family supported the Lancastrian side in the Wars of the Roses and were active
military leaders in the Hundred Years War with France.

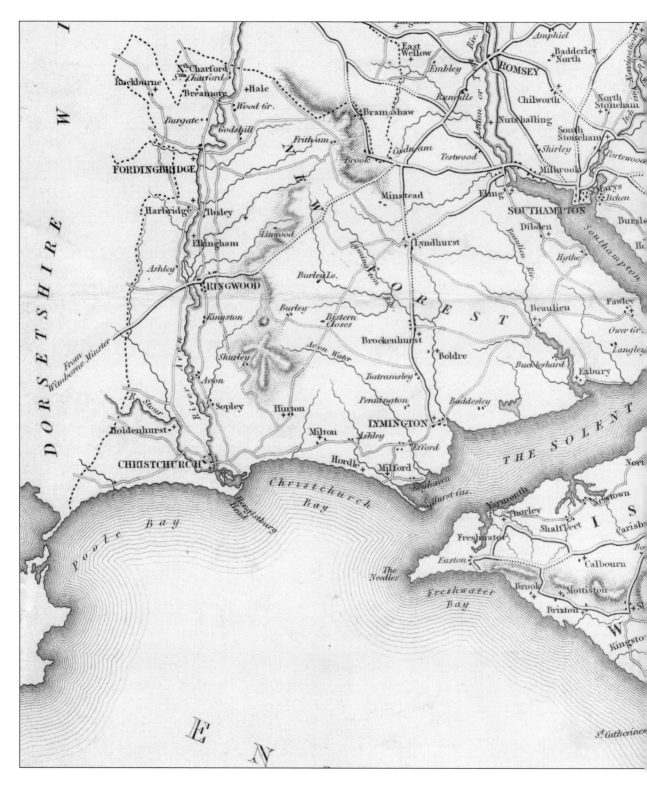

HAMPSHIRE COUNTY
MAP SHOWING
CHRISTCHURCH AND
SURROUNDING AREAS
c1838

THE CIVIL WAR

The Civil War began in April 1642. During the war, a Parliamentary garrison occupied Hurst but Christchurch was held for the King. Christchurch saw no action until after General Waller's Parliamentary victory at Cheriton in 1644. In April of that year, a detachment from Waller's army surprised 22 of the King's recruiting officers in Christchurch and captured 100 horse and 400 foot soldiers without needing to fight; although, the 'valiant oyster women petitioner' wanted to put up a fight. Later in 1644 the Royalist cavalry commander, General Goreing, sought to recapture Christchurch, but was driven off.

On 15 January, 1645, Goreing made a determined attempt on Christchurch. However, the garrison had made preparations: gun platforms were erected on the north and south sides of the motte, which was raised to command the town and the quay. In order to give a clear field of fire, houses were pulled down.

Goreing's men drove the Parliamentary troops out of the external defences, into the priory, churchyard and castle, where they stood a three-day, close siege. Claims for damage were being argued for many years after the war. A ghost in a Bridge Street garden has been reported as wearing Civil War armour. The defenders lit a beacon on top of the keep to attract help from Poole. The garrison commander loaded his surplus gunpowder into a boat, and sent it by night to Yarmouth, on the Isle of Wight. The cavaliers found the castle too hard to take and drew off into the New Forest.

In the meantime, the commander at Yarmouth sent a force to Lymington where, reinforced by the troops there, they marched to Christchurch and its relief. The cavaliers narrowly missed being cut off and made good their retreat. The Parliamentary commander at Christchurch was rewarded by promotion.

By 1650, the defences were an embarrassment: the castle had canons but there was no garrison, so the guns were removed. The castle was not mined, as an explosion in the town centre would have wrecked the place. About 1656 the north and south walls of the keep were pulled down.

After the Parliamentary capture of Christchurch, the Church

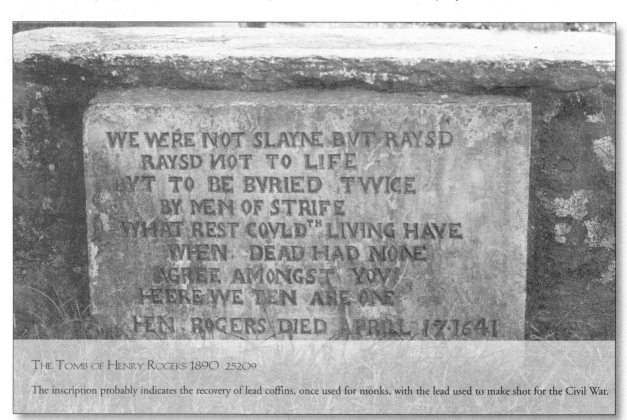

THE TOMB OF HENRY ROGERS 1890 25209

The inscription probably indicates the recovery of lead coffins, once used for monks, with the lead used to make shot for the Civil War.

THE CIVIL WAR

MILLHAMS STREET, THE CONGREGATIONAL CHURCH 1900 45054

Nonconformists were ejected from the Priory Church in 1660 when Charles II was restored. They continued their worship in various places such as St Catherine's Hill, but in 1816 built a church on this site. The church in the photograph, and its adjoining church hall, was built in 1867. It became the United Reformed Church but has since been sold to the Elim Church.

of England vicar was put out of his living until the Restoration in 1660. The Puritan vicar then lost his living. Nonconformists met in secret on St Catherine's Hill and in private houses, until things became calmer. The stoning of the Sheriff (Shire Reeve) in 1663, and threats to the life of the mayor demonstrated the violence of

instruments of public punishment. These included: stocks, pillory, ducking stool, whirly-gig, manacles, and the gibbet at Parley on the old county boundary.

The Earl of Clarendon, historian of the Civil War, had great plans when he became Lord of the Manor: to develop Christchurch Harbour as a port - this involved making a new entrance through

Mudeford Sandspit. This soon silted up but the Clarendon Rocks, remains of the works, are still visible at low tides.

In 1664, The River Avon Navigation Act was passed; it is still on the Statute Book. The Avon was to be rendered navigable, to carry cargo to Salisbury. The work was completed by 1682. Up to about

Salisbury.

The Avon at Christchurch has two channels; thus creating a low island crossed by Bridge Street. The Town Bridge was built in the 15th or 16th century. The noise of pipes and drums, played by ghostly pilgrims passing over Town Bridge, has been reported.

SMUGGLING

For many generations, the main industry in Christchurch was smuggling. Duty was raised on exports, as well as imports; a vital tax for the Crown was the export duty on wool. Local smugglers were called 'owlers', perhaps derived from 'woolers'.

The Customs Commissioners set up a Waterguard in 1698, to operate rowboats in harbours such as Christchurch, and sailing cutters from larger harbours. Riding Officers patrolled the coast on horseback; several were based at Christchurch under a Supervisor in Bridge Street. 'Free Trade' goods were run across the channel in shallow draft luggers, designed to be able to run up on the shore and unload direct. Smugglers also used deep keel cutters, capable of great speed, but requiring their cargo to be unloaded into smaller boats to get it ashore. Galleys were built to smuggle bullion as an export: they could row into the wind and so escape a sailing boat. Smugglers fought violently to avoid capture, since the risk was not so much prison as impressment into the Royal Navy. The risks of capture were not great: smuggling luggers, unloading to a gang of 300 men, would not expect interference from a rowboat with seven men, or a single Riding Officer. Even revenue cutters with a crew of two dozen men, or more, could be told to clear off - or words to that effect.

Smugglers in Christchurch kidnapped a youth, and sent him abroad, as a slave, in order to terrify his family into silence. Even worse, a Riding Officer from Christchurch was beaten to death on his own doorstep, in front of his wife and children. Romantic tales about smugglers conceal the truth of their brutality.

An example of romantic fiction, about local smugglers, is the tale of 'Hookey's Hole'. Samuel Hookey was a local smuggler who lived at Wick. The story is that on 29 August 1796, when Hookey was 71 years of age, he drowned in the Stour at Wick, fleeing from revenue men. He was supposed to have drowned because he was wearing a money belt full of golden guineas. The name Hookey's Hole was given to the bar at the holiday camp. Skindivers sought the gold in the river in 1954. Unfortunately, the whole tale is fiction: a local resident made up the story to justify the name of the bar.

The Battle of Mudeford took place on the evening of Saturday 16 July 1784. Two luggers had loaded a cargo with 42,000 gallons of spirit and 8 tons of tea. The luggers arrived near Christchurch Harbour on 14 July, and they were observed by the excise cutter, Resolution, which sent in a boat. The smugglers warned off the

WICK FERRY HOLIDAY CAMP AND THE RIVER STOUR c1955 C99131

Rowboats for hire cluster next to the ferry landing.

SMUGGLING

'CROSSING THE LINE', WICK FERRY HOLIDAY CAMP C1955 C99150

King Neptune, with his trident and his court, at a mock 'Crossing the Line' ceremony.

SMUGGLING

boat's crew. The Resolution then sent her boat to search for HMS Orestes, which was co-operating with the revenue, while she sailed to search for the Swan - a customs cutter, whose captain was brother to the captain of the Resolution. The three Crown vessels met, off Christchurch Ledge, on 16 July.

The smugglers had unloaded their cargo and stacked it for removal near the Haven at Mudeford. The local Supervisor of Riding Officers, Joshua Jeans, was a man who had been four times mayor, had a daughter married to the vicar of Christchurch and two sons – one a doctor, the other a priest; he was also in league with the smugglers. Jeans sent one of his officers to the Haven, to ensure their share of 'the crop' was put to one side for collection. These tubs of spirit would enable them to report some as seizures and so appear to show that they were functioning properly.

The smugglers observed the arrival of the two revenue cutters and HMS Orestes - an 18-gun sloop, with a crew totalling 94 men. The smugglers ashore were 300 to 400 men-strong, with over 40 wagons and 300 horses, plus the crew of the luggers, perhaps a total of 500 men. They realised they could not hope for the luggers to escape, so they prepared to defend the entrance to the harbour, to allow time to get the cargo away.

Meanwhile the Crown vessels sent in their ships' boats in a cutting-out expedition. The six boats rowed up the Run, to force the harbour entrance. However, they came under fire from the shore. The navy

GAMES AT WICK FERRY HOLIDAY CAMP c1955
C99136

This early holiday camp used beach hut-type villas. Seaside holidays became available to a wider range of customers, thanks in part to the motorcar

Smuggling

'HOOKEY'S HOLE', WICK FERRY HOLIDAY CAMP C1955
C99179

Samuel Hookey was an 18th-century smuggler. The fable of his
being drowned with a money belt of golden guineas gave rise to the
story of Hookey's Hole.

had casualties, and the second in command of Orestes was mortally
wounded. The boats were driven off and kept out of the harbour
for three hours. The Christchurch Riding Officers reported to the
Supervisor, Joshua Jeans, at 10 Bridge Street, for orders. He told them
that he was going to bed and advised them to do the same.

The smugglers and their cargo escaped, but the Master of Orestes
died the next day. There was a great scandal from killing a naval
officer; Jeans was dismissed from the service. A reward of £200
was offered; three smugglers were charged and one was hung in
London. It was notoriously difficult to get any local court to convict
a smuggler.

In 1792, work began on a barracks in the Portfield, to
accommodate half a troop of light cavalry. This barracks was not
to put down smuggling but to resist the threatened Napoleonic
invasion. The first occupants were the South Hants Militia. The
cavalry arrived in 1795 and were initially feared, but the town soon
appreciated their buoyant effect on the economy. The Royal Horse
Artillery, and their guns, soon succeeded the 20th Light Dragoons.
There were several local volunteer units: Christchurch Loyal
Volunteer Artillery, a Company of Militia, a Troop of Yeomanry
Cavalry, and Sea Fencibles.

Paupers, born locally, were able to seek support in the 'poor
house', which was originally operated by the church. A wife could
enter the poor house of her husband's parish but the sexes had
separate dormitories. A widow had to return to the Poor House
of her parish of birth, even if it was hundreds of miles away. A
barn was purchased in 1745 for conversion to a workhouse; this
eventually became The Red House, which is now a museum.

SMUGGLING

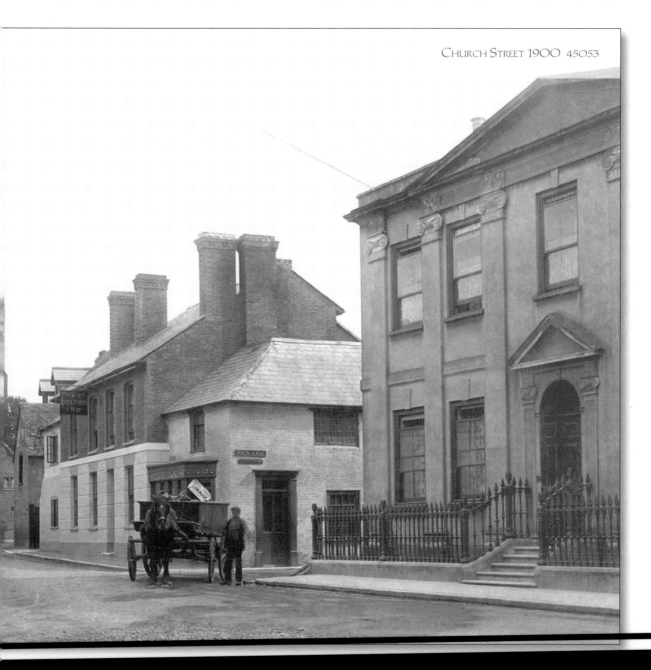

also a smuggler. A naval officer (the younger brother of the diplomat who built the second High Cliff mansion that gave its name to Highcliffe) captured her. He placed the young woman in his mother's house at Bure, but she was packed off, out of the way, to London, and became a servant in a brothel. She ended

... as the mistress of the Duc de Bourbon, last Prince de Condé, and in 1818 became the Baroness de Feucheres. She returned to England and built Bure Homage mansion at Mudeford.

Another local female smuggler was Lovey Warn, who would carry goods ashore wrapped around her body, or in bladders hung under

SMUGGLING

her cloths. In one known case, the revenue arrived to search the Eight Bells in Church Street, and a tub of smuggled spirits had just been delivered. A woman hurriedly sat on the tub, concealing it under her skirts, while she washed a baby. The Officers left without a seizure. The Eight Bells was named for the seven bells of the Priory; it was the 'nineteenth hole' for the bell-ringers. The Priory now has a peal of 12 bells.

After the defeat of France, the Royal Navy was used to blockade the coast, and so gain the upper hand over the smugglers. The Coastguard was set up as 'Preventive Men' to put down smuggling but also became involved in rescue work. The Lloyds insurance market paid for a lifeboat to be stationed at Christchurch in 1802 and in 1805, Mr Rose of Mudeford, offered to pay for a lifeboat. In 1870, the Christchurch Times reported the first services of another new lifeboat. The Royal National Lifeboat Institution stationed an inshore lifeboat at Mudeford in 1963; since 1936 a private rescue boat had been operating - the owner was awarded the RNLI Silver Medal.

The first ever RNLI Gold Medal for gallantry was awarded in 1824, for a service at Mudeford. A Coastguard Officer, Lt Cdr Freemantle RN, swam out with a line, through breaking seas, to a brig that had been driven onto the Sand Bar. The vessel broke up in the surf and the crew were saved, although Freemantle was nearly drowned. In 1870, a Silver Medal was given to another officer for a rescue at Boscombe, west of Christchurch.

THE PRIORY CHURCH FROM QUAY ROAD C1965
C99240

This churchyard is where smugglers carried their cargo from the quay one Sunday morning, past the congregation.

MUDEFORD, THE HAVEN QUAY c1955 M106011

The 17th-century Dutch Cottages and the original Haven Inn are shown. The picture looks towards the present site of the RNLI Lifeboat Station. In July 1784 these buildings saw smugglers beat off a cutting-out expedition, by the Royal Navy and Customs & Excise.

SMUGGLING

MUDEFORD, THE RUN 1918
68057

This picture is taken from the Sandspit; the Black House on the right was once the home of the Shipyard Manager. A salmon punt, used as a ferry, is moored in the Run. A crane at Mudeford Quay was used for unloading barges. The buildings on the quay, on the left, are the Dutch Cottages, so-called because in the 17th century they were occupied by Dutch dredging experts. The building in the centre was the original Haven Inn: defended by smugglers, in 1784, against the Royal Navy. The building on the right on the quay is the 19th-century Haven Inn.

MUDEFORD, THE HAVEN C1955 M106035

The picture shows Christchurch Harbour, east of the Run. The River Mude flows into the harbour, on the left and the Bure Stream enters on the right. The remains of a Roman vessel were excavated here in 1910. There are a wide variety of small, privately owned, pleasure craft in the scene. A typical salmon punt is in the centre foreground; two others are moored centre left, with their nets piled in the stern ready for use. A sea-fishing boat is moored on the left, in the background. Mudeford is still a registered sea-fishing harbour, and fish can be purchased on the quay.

SMUGGLING

CHURCH STREET, LOOKING NORTH C1955 C99146

SMUGGLING

The extension of the High Street shown in view 45053 (pages 60-61) has changed direction: it has curved on the left, to avoid the castle ditch. When the Castle Tavern (on the left opposite the Dolphin site) was converted to a pub in the 1980s (it is now Soho wine bar), a ghostly mist emerged and then disappeared through the floor, as it followed the slope of the ditch. The street is now largely given over to restaurants and fancy goods shops, serving the tourist trade. On the right, between Church Lane and the Priory, is the Eight Bells - a pub until 1907. Between Church and Wick Lanes is the Dolphin Inn, rebuilt in 1864 after a fire, then demolished for redevelopment in 1973. The large Palladian-style mansion, on the right of the picture and overlooking the Market Place, is Square House: built in 1776 by John Cook, a wealthy brewer who owned the brewery next door in Wick Lane, and controlled some 20 pubs. Cook owned a sloop: 'The Stour', which smuggled 34,000 gallons of spirit in July 1784. He was mayor five times. Square House was demolished in 1958.

Church Street has changed: it now has more cars and shops (see C99120 below). The Bournemouth Corporation trolley bus is emerging from the turntable at the Dolphin yard. This turntable has been retained and is probably the only one left in the country. Trams had been replaced in 1936; trolley buses ceased to operate in 1969.

The Market Place (see C99146 left) was once in the road, in front of Burton's the tailors. The Market Hall – Town Hall, stood here until 1859. On the right is Ye Olde George Inn (once the George and Dragon Inn) in Castle Street; it has a ghost. The parked cars show yellow lines and traffic wardens had not yet been invented.

CHURCH STREET, TROLLEY BUS, EMERGING FROM TURNTABLE c1955 C99120

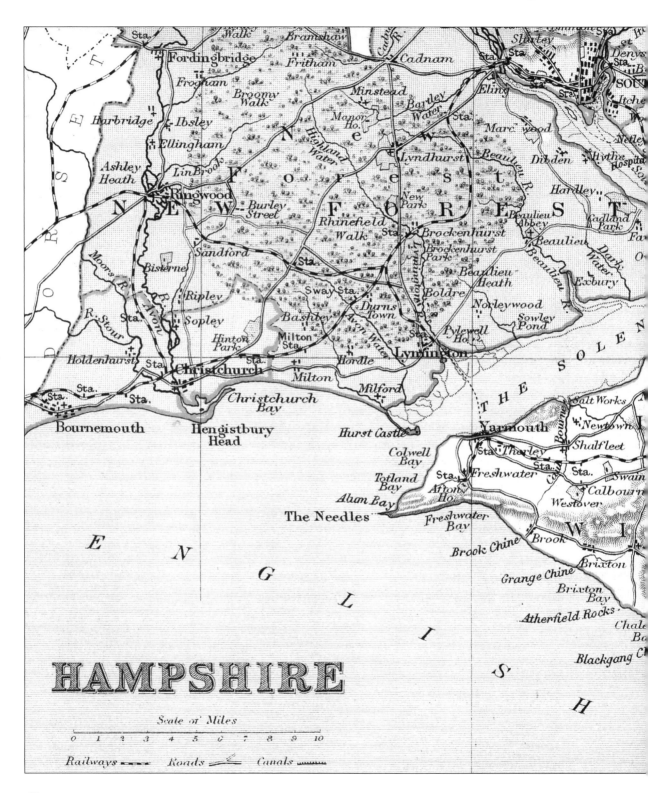

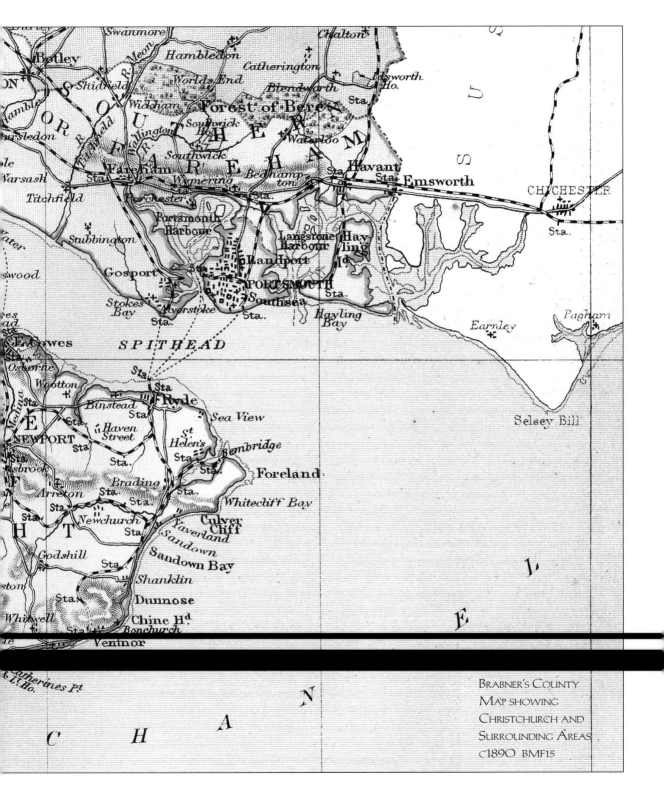

BRABNER'S COUNTY
MAP SHOWING
CHRISTCHURCH AND
SURROUNDING AREAS
c1890 BMF15

Victorian Times

A most important development in the history of Christchurch was the arrival of the railway. This first reached Holmesley (known as Christchurch Road) in 1847. The railway did not reach Christchurch, via Ringwood, until 1862. The railway gave the opportunity for perishable goods to be sent to distant markets. The construction of a rail link through Brockenhurst in 1888, cut out the change at Ringwood. The railway permitted the transport of heavy goods in bulk. Most of all, the railway gave freedom of rapid movement from distant places, giving rise to the tourist trade and the need for hotels. Many visitors liked the area so much, they returned to live there on their retirement. The arrival of the railway also brought about the development of bus links.

The small boys, on the left of view 45043 (see right), are wearing knickerbocker trousers, heavy boots, wide collars and cloth caps, as is the baker's boy on the right. The street surface shows the signs of horse traffic and the carts of everyday transport are visible. The town pump, on the left, is now long gone.

On the left is the drapers (mercers) shop of G F Ferrey and Son, now Bookends Bookshop, and originally owned by a mercer who founded Clingan's Charity in 1736. This charity still exists and helps equip young people in finding work. The Ferrey family also operated as tailors, milliners and undertakers from 1760 until 1936, when the effect of chain stores helped drive such independents out of business. The casualties of World War I also affected them; the eldest son was killed at the Dardenelles and the youngest lost a leg in France.

At the end of the High Street can be seen Brewery House (demolished 1954), projecting into the road at the point where the Bargate stood (removed 1724). Beyond, in the background, is the Antelope Hotel, which stood on an island of houses, at the junction where Fountain roundabout is now. The latter was named after the Fountain Hotel, which replaced the Wagon and Horses Inn. Opposite were Hodges and Mason's cycle shop (1902-37), and The Green Tree Inn - burnt down in 1863. All were demolished in 1953 to make way for the by-pass, which is no such thing since it splits the town in two. Until the by-pass, High Street was the main east-to-west route, between Southampton and Bournemouth.

The turret building on the right, with the flag, is the Town Hall, which was originally built in the Market Place in 1745, but moved to its present site in 1859. In 1902, a Technical School was

VICTORIAN TIMES

HIGH STREET 1900 45043

VICTORIAN TIMES

HIGH STREET, THE JUNCTION WITH CASTLE STREET c1955   C99145

The signpost to Lyndhurst, in the foreground of this photograph, stands where the Town Hall presided over the market. Many buildings in this photograph have now gone, or have changed use: the High Street has been penetrated by financial services, also by cafes aimed at visitors. Much of the shopping has been driven to out-of-town supermarkets. Fortunately, many of the shop fronts have been preserved.

built behind the hall, and later converted to council offices. It was demolished in 1979 and replaced by new offices in Bridge Street. The Town Hall was then restored with the mayor's parlour on the first floor and the ground floor as a market shelter. It is known that an earlier market building stood at the southeast side of High Street at junction with Millhams, this was known as the Toll House. The flat-roofed building, with a wide shop awning, south of the Ship Inn was once a Protestant Dissenters School; this closed when seven of its pupils were drowned in one day. Behind this side of the street was once Cox's Fusee chain factory and Mitchell's Brewery.

The shop sign, 'Haywards', is visible on the centre-right of the picture, and it was a jewellers shop and watchmakers who used locally manufactured fusee chains. Haywards was also a registry office for domestic servants. The shop on the right, with wrought-iron decoration, is that of Tucker and Son: booksellers, stationers, family grocers and tea dealers - it closed in 1958.

The growth in the railway attracted river fishermen to enjoy the famous salmon fishery of the Royalty and Avon and the fishery at Throop on the Stour. The sea fishery at Mudeford Haven continued to be important, as did the salmon netting. The Rams Horn net dates from Saxon times, and is still in use. Every year 'Blessing of the Waters' is carried out on Rogation Sunday from a boat in the Run. There was also shipbuilding at Mudeford; in the 1850s 300 ton vessels were built on the Sandspit.

Another important local industry was the manufacture of fusee chain for watches. It is not known how the industry first came to the area, but it was taken up as suitable employment for paupers at the workhouse and factory workers. Some 500 women were employed on this work, which required great concentration. The women may have visited the wells at Purewell and Tutton's Well, as they had reputations for curative properties, and were still used for such purposes up to the beginning of the 20th century.

VICTORIAN TIMES

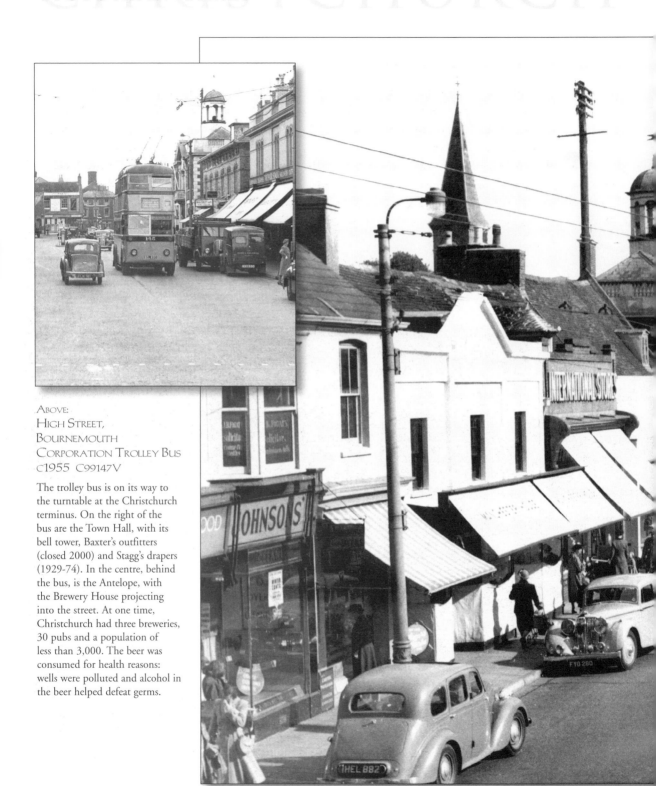

ABOVE:
HIGH STREET,
BOURNEMOUTH
CORPORATION TROLLEY BUS
c1955 C99147V

The trolley bus is on its way to the turntable at the Christchurch terminus. On the right of the bus are the Town Hall, with its bell tower, Baxter's outfitters (closed 2000) and Stagg's drapers (1929-74). In the centre, behind the bus, is the Antelope, with the Brewery House projecting into the street. At one time, Christchurch had three breweries, 30 pubs and a population of less than 3,000. The beer was consumed for health reasons: wells were polluted and alcohol in the beer helped defeat germs.

HIGH STREET, LOOKING SOUTH c1955   C99143

The double-decker bus is a Hants and Dorset vehicle, on the route to Bournemouth. The white building, on the left of the International Stores, was once Payne's drapers, which became Barclays Bank in the 1960s; in World War I it was a Union Jack Club. The International had been the site of Williams's grocers from 1845-94; the building was pulled down in the 1970s. Next to it and the Town Hall, was a 14th-century building known as 'Hookey's House', demolished in 1973. On the right of the picture is a flat roof, below which were the District Bank and the Westminster Bank. Beyond, in front of the trees, was the Masonic Hengist Lodge, opened in 1837 - now a solicitors office. Next to the trees is the 1864 home of James Druitt, now the Druitt Public Library. Out of sight is the 1934 Woolworth's store where ghostly figures have been seen walking through the wall to the Corn Factors next door; faces were reported appearing at the windows of this empty building, but the windows are now boarded up.

THE OLD SAILING CLUB AND CHRISTCHURCH QUAY
C1960 C99226

The former Sailing Club building remains but the club has moved. The large building behind the old clubhouse was Elkins Boatyard where small naval craft were built. A Tuckton to Mudeford ferry lies at the quay.

The railway had been an engine for change in the 19th century. Transportation continued to be an engine for social change in the 20th century, with motor vehicles and aircraft. However, the major impetus for change was war. Women took over jobs, hitherto male preserves. The suffragettes' battle for the vote was won through the casualty lists from Flanders. The sacrifice of local men is recorded on the War Memorial at Purewell, in the Chapel of Remembrance at the Priory and the Rolls of Honour kept by the Council.

A mounting reputation that they were healthy places for holidays and retirement helped the New Forest and Bournemouth to grow.

THE BOAT HIRE
PONTOON AT
CHRISTCHURCH
QUAY c1960
C99255

The view is up the River
Stour to Pontins Holiday
Camp (now developed
for housing).

The increasing availability of private motorcars, motor coaches and bus routes, together with the railway, gave people access to the coast, as never before. Hotels, bed and breakfast, as well as restaurants and cafes of all descriptions, offered employment and increased the wealth of the town. The years of 1939/45 saw a hardening of Importance from German-occupied France and Channel Isles. Many of the same vulnerable points would have been recognised in previous wars with European powers. D Company, 7th Battalion Hampshire Territorials, reported to the Portfield drill hall in 1939, and was embodied for the duration of hostilities.

Christchurch town was to be defended by E Company, 7th (Boscombe) Home Guard Battalion Hampshire Regiment, as an anti-tank island. The defence was based on the railway, which was lined with anti-tank obstacles, supported by pillboxes. There were also Convent Meadows, the Old Sailing Club, Wick Ferry and between the rivers, the Mill Stream and marshes, as in Saxon times. Because this promontory defence mirrored that at Hengistbury and the Saxon burgh, after the war part of it was scheduled as an ancient monument. The monument, Dorset AM832, is Britain's most 'modern' ancient monument. The Home Guard HQ was at 10 Bridge Street, the site of the Riding Officers HQ in the 18th century.

A Weir on The Stour c1955
C99401

The fisherman is on part of Christchurch Borough's, Iford Golf Course. On the left horizon is Ramsdown, to the right is Blackwater Hill; between the hills passes Wessex Way, the Bournemouth to Ringwood motorway.

House Boats on The Stour, Converted from Naval Motor Launches
c1955 C99154

These craft lie opposite Wick Ferry Holiday Camp, on the Bournemouth bank. Such motor launches were of the type built at Elkins Boatyard.

Scaffolding, barbed wire, pillboxes, and mines to cover the beaches defended the shore. These defences were protected from airborne attack from the rear by using the railway line, and roadblocks with pillboxes, to cover bridges. All bridges were prepared for demolition, including the ancient Town and Waterloo Bridges.

The Experimental Bridging Establishment, at Christchurch Barracks, had an important role: it was there that the famous Bailey bridge was invented. It also held Experimental Demolition and Tunnelling Establishments. Troops were billeted on civilian families, as were evacuees from city centres. For a time, after Dunkirk, General Montgomery had his headquarters at Shortwood House, Magdalen Lane.

An emergency beach battery was set up at Steamer Point, Mudeford, and another at Hengistbury. There were mobile anti-aircraft batteries at Southborne, Hurn, Ramsdown and Holmsley.

RAF Hurn Airfield was opened in January 1941; in 1945-6 it was the nation's main airfield for foreign flights, until Heathrow opened. This airfield, in Christchurch, is now Bournemouth International Airport and an important part of the local economy. The first underground Ground Control Interception Centre at Sopley opened early in 1941. It controlled the destruction of 100 enemy aircraft. RAF Holmsley South opened in 1942. The Royal Observer Corps had a post at Twynham School. The RAF had VHF direction finders at Ramsdown and St Catherine's Hill.

Christchurch Airfield, at Somerford, had opened in 1926 as a flying club; it became RAF Christchurch. The Air Defence Experimental Establishment was at Somerford and Steamer Point; before the war it gave rise to rumours of death rays (radar experiments). The Signals Research and Development Establishment later replaced it. In 1941, Airspeed's shadow factory was opened at Somerford, and during the war it built Oxford aircraft and Mosquito fighter-bombers for the RAF, and Horsa gliders for the army. Also at Somerford was HMS Raven, a Fleet Air Arm gliders for the army. Also at Somerford was stationed there to support the invasion of Normandy. Others were at the Advanced Landing Ground at Winkton.

The RAF also had a detachment of the secret 80 Wing at Hengistbury. Their role was to detect and plot German air navigation transmissions: to determine targets and hence warn the defences. They also jammed the transmissions, or bent them, so that

THE TWENTIETH CENTURY

the German bombers attacked open countryside.

Civil defence was managed from the Air Raid Precautions Incident Control Centre at the council offices (now Saxon Square). Christchurch Control Centre received a total of 3,596 air-raid warnings, of which 957 were alerts; 1,008 properties were damaged excluding broken glass, four civilians were killed and 23 wounded by enemy raiders. More civilians were killed by accidents due to blackout, mines and crashing allied aircraft: the worst case killed 17 and injured 13.

Local war manufacturers included Elkins Boatyard at Convent Meadows, where small vessels were produced for the Royal Navy. As in World War I, women took men's jobs, even more so with Government direction of labour.

The war made propaganda essential, and the cinema was next to radio in importance for mass communication. Christchurch had cinemas; the first was a private one set up in a garage near Waterloo Bridge in 1911. The first public cinema was in 1914, at Bargates; in 1946 it became the club for The Royal British Legion. The Regent Cinema, in High Street, was opened in 1931 and closed in the 1980s in favour of bingo; it is now a community arts centre. The stalls have a pair of ghosts.

In 1951, The Red House was opened as a museum in Quay Road - it too is supposed to be haunted. This former workhouse has extensive collections of local history. There is also an active Christchurch Local History Society, based at the Druitt Library in High Street.

Post-war building development has created an urban area along the coast, from New Milton in Hampshire to Upton, west of Poole. Much development was on heath or agricultural land but in Christchurch it meant the loss of several old buildings, like Square House. The losses include some views of the Priory, which have been obstructed by development. The Council now recognises that the borough's unique selling proposition is heritage.

THE TWENTIETH CENTURY

GROVE FARM CARAVAN PARK c1955 C99191

The River Stour runs across the land behind the caravans. On the right of the horizon is St Catherine's Hill, left of which are Blackwater and Ramsdown Hills. The caravan park still operates with much-improved facilities.

THE TWENTIETH CENTURY

THE RIVER STOUR
C1960 C99218

The Stour at Grove Farm
Caravan Park, with Cattle
on the Holdenhurst Bank.
The caravan park has fishing
rights available.

ORDNANCE SURVEY MAP

ORDNANCE SURVEY MAP

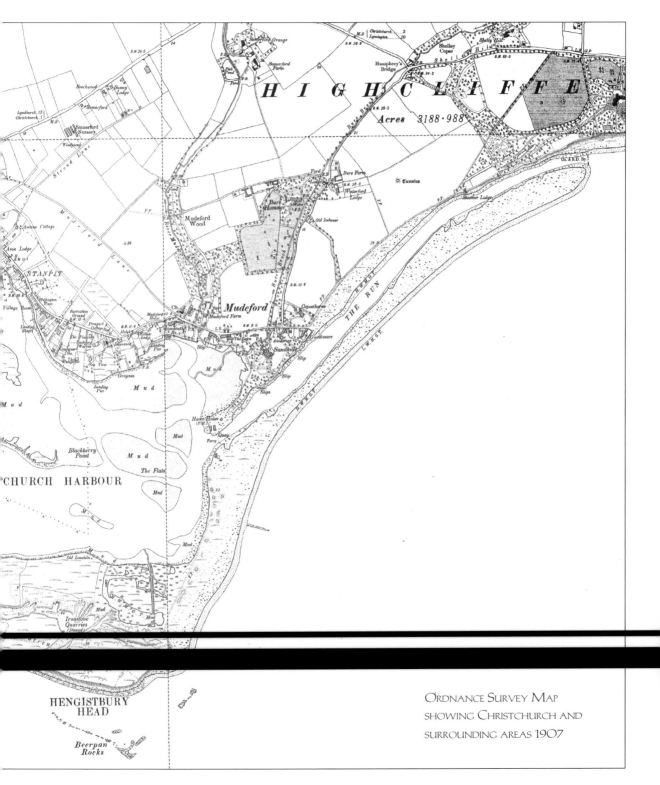

ORDNANCE SURVEY MAP
SHOWING CHRISTCHURCH AND
SURROUNDING AREAS 1907

Names of Pre-Publication Buyers

The following people have kindly supported this book by purchasing limited edition copies prior to publication.

Mick Alexander, Christchurch
The Ashby Family, Christchurch
Moore Ballinger & Polo of Christchurch
To Mum, Margaret Bannister, 'Happy Birthday'
Jill & Norman Barnes, Christchurch
Mr M G & Mrs S Y Bayliss, Christchurch
Derek Michael J Blake, Christchurch
Philip John Bostock
Mr S R & Mrs C L S Bowden, Christchurch
Mr D J Bowmer, Christchurch
In memory of my parents & 3 brothers, E Brady
The Brennan-Pope Family, Christchurch
Mayze Bridell & John Bridell
The Brolan & Awbery Families of Christchurch
Mr R M & Mrs J Brown, Christchurch
The Cafe Family, Christchurch
Brian & Annabel Cameron, Christchurch
Mr W A & Mrs D W Campbell, Christchurch
The Carter-Blandford Family, Christchurch
In memory of the Chalk & Ford Families
Thelma: In memory of Daddy, Harry Cheater
The Chorley Family, Christchurch
John & Brenda Clarke, Barton on Sea
In memory of Margaret Cobb
John M Cole & Rozanne Cole, Christchurch
Caroline Butcher Cousens, Christchurch
The Croucher Family of Christchurch
Mark H Crowston & Family, Christchurch
Carrie Davies, In memory of Joanne
Mr & Mrs R E Day, Christchurch
To Debbie with love on our wedding, David
Dione & John Denton, Highcliffe
Donald Dow 1955
The Downer Family, Burton
In memory of E & F Edmunds, Christchurch
Mr F & Mrs D Esterling, Christchurch
Phil & Doreen Fowler
Tom Fradley and Eileen Clegg
Cyril Frampton, 'Happy Birthday Dad', Feb 2005
In memory of Edith Fugatt, Christchurch
The Fugatt Family, Christchurch
The Gazzard Family, Mudeford
Georgina & Trevor 'For their birthdays'
I R & H A C Goodall, Christchurch
To Gerry Guest on his 70th Birthday
Mr S P Hancock & Mrs K L Hancock, Christchurch
In memory of George Harris, Highcliffe
Edna Harriss, Christchurch
In memory of Doug & Malcolm Hawkins
The Hayter-Dumbrill Family, Christchurch
Jacqueline Butcher Hitchen, Christchurch
In memory of our friends from the river
Happy 60th Birthday Jenny
Spencer Johnson, Burton, Christchurch

Todd Johnson, Christchurch
Mr M J Keeping & Mrs M J Keeping, Christchurch
To Bob Kerley, Bransgore, from the Kids
Margaret J King
In memory of Nan King, Christchurch
Tenth Anniversary of Robert & Nicola Lehmann
Mr W J & Mrs J E Liddle, Christchurch
Mr Kim Lowe & Family, Bournemouth
Mr Kenneth W Ludlow & Mrs Anne Ludlow
Tim McKay & Family, Southbourne
The Mann Family, Christchurch
Mark & Sue 28 January 2002
Ian & Elizabeth Messer, Christchurch
Birthday Wishes Mike from Moeke and Bay
Happy Memories of Mum & Dad, M & R Millis
Steve, Lisa, Phil & Nichola Mitchell
Mam, Dad, Chris, Roger, Russ Moore & Nanny
In memory of John S C Morgan, past Mayor
To Mum & Dad, Happy 45th Wedding Anniversary from
   all of us.
Happy Anniversary Mum & Dad 31 March 2005, from
   Adrian, Ruth, Ben and Daniel
In memory of Kath Pardy, Christchurch
Tom Pateman, Christchurch
Gilbert Payton, Christchurch
In memory of Nap & Ruth Pearsons
Barbara Percival
Philip Puncher, Mudeford
Happy Anniversary Lyn Raftery, from Tony
The Roots Family of Mudeford
Mr & Mrs D F Sampson, Christchurch
The Saunders Family, Christchurch
Tina Sikes, Christchurch
On your 21st Birthday Lee Singleton, love Gran
Gary & Janice Slater of Christchurch
Mr W & Mrs P V Temple, Hurn
In memory of W Topp, The Butcher, Bargates
Nancy & Sid Walker
Mike & Stella Ward, Highcliffe
Mr & Mrs S J Warren & Families, Christchurch
The Whatson Family, Christchurch
Mr & Mrs Gordon Way, Christchurch
Graham White; Nursery Manager CBC 41 years
The Wickson Family, Highcliffe
John L B Wild
S G & A A Wilkinson
Ann Lavinia Willett
Amanda C Williams, Highcliffe-on-Sea
Elizabeth Williams, Brussels
The Williams Family, Bure Homage
Janet Williams, March 2005
Tony & Christine Williams, Highcliffe
Irene Anne Mary Wright
Tribute to dear Arnold, Sylvia Youngson

INDEX

Hurn Road...10

Blackwater Ferry..10-11

Bridge Street...38-39

Castle Bailey.........................28-29, 30, 31, 32-33

Castle Street...................................34-35, 36-37

Christchurch Quay......16-17, 18, 20-21, 22, 76-77

Church Street.......................................64,66-67

Congregational Church................................55

Convent Walk......................................22, 24-25

Grove Farm Caravan Park.........................80-81

High Street...70-75

Mill Stream..38

Mudeford..............................60-61, 62-63, 64-65

Place Mill...23

Priory..........................14,19, 26-27, 38, 40-51, 62

River Stour......................................15, 18, 78-79

Town Bridge..39

Wick Ferry Holiday Camp...................56-59, 60

Frith Book Co Titles

www.francisfrith.co.uk

The Frith Book Company publishes over 100 new titles each year. A selection of those currently available is listed below. For latest catalogue please contact Frith Book Co.
Town Books 96 pages, approximately 100 photos. **County and Themed Books** 128 pages, approximately 150 photos (unless specified). All titles hardback with laminated case and jacket, except those indicated pb (paperback)

Amersham, Chesham & Rickmansworth (pb)	1-85937-340-2	£9.99	Devon (pb)	1-85937-297-x	£9.99
Andover (pb)	1-85937-292-9	£9.99	Devon Churches (pb)	1-85937-250-3	£9.99
Aylesbury (pb)	1-85937-227-9	£9.99	Dorchester (pb)	1-85937-307-0	£9.99
Barnstaple (pb)	1-85937-300-3	£9.99	Dorset (pb)	1-85937-269-4	£9.99
Basildon Living Memories (pb)	1-85937-515-4	£9.99	Dorset Coast (pb)	1-85937-299-6	£9.99
Bath (pb)	1-85937-419-0	£9.99	Dorset Living Memories (pb)	1-85937-584-7	£9.99
Bedford (pb)	1-85937-205-8	£9.99	Down the Severn (pb)	1-85937-560-x	£9.99
Bedfordshire Living Memories	1-85937-513-8	£14.99	Down The Thames (pb)	1-85937-278-3	£9.99
Belfast (pb)	1-85937-303-8	£9.99	Down the Trent	1-85937-311-9	£14.99
Berkshire (pb)	1-85937-191-4	£9.99	East Anglia (pb)	1-85937-265-1	£9.99
Berkshire Churches	1-85937-170-1	£17.99	East Grinstead (pb)	1-85937-138-8	£9.99
Berkshire Living Memories	1-85937-332-1	£14.99	East London	1-85937-080-2	£14.99
Black Country	1-85937-497-2	£12.99	East Sussex (pb)	1-85937-606-1	£9.99
Blackpool (pb)	1-85937-393-3	£9.99	Eastbourne (pb)	1-85937-399-2	£9.99
Bognor Regis (pb)	1-85937-431-x	£9.99	Edinburgh (pb)	1-85937-193-0	£8.99
Bournemouth (pb)	1-85937-545-6	£9.99	England In The 1880s	1-85937-331-3	£17.99
Bradford (pb)	1-85937-204-x	£9.99	Essex - Second Selection	1-85937-456-5	£14.99
Bridgend (pb)	1-85937-386-0	£7.99	Essex (pb)	1-85937-270-8	£9.99
Bridgwater (pb)	1-85937-305-4	£9.99	Essex Coast	1-85937-342-9	£14.99
Bridport (pb)	1-85937-327-5	£9.99	Essex Living Memories	1-85937-490-5	£14.99
Brighton (pb)	1-85937-192-2	£8.99	Exeter	1-85937-539-1	£9.99
Bristol (pb)	1-85937-264-3	£9.99	Exmoor (pb)	1-85937-608-8	£9.99
British Life A Century Ago (pb)	1-85937-213-9	£9.99	Falmouth (pb)	1-85937-594-4	£9.99
Buckinghamshire (pb)	1-85937-200-7	£9.99	Folkestone (pb)	1-85937-124-8	£9.99
Camberley (pb)	1-85937-222-8	£9.99	Frome (pb)	1-85937-317-8	£9.99
Cambridge (pb)	1-85937-422-0	£9.99	Glamorgan	1-85937-488-3	£14.99
Cambridgeshire (pb)	1-85937-420-4	£9.99	Glasgow (pb)	1-85937-190-6	£9.99
Cambridgeshire Villages	1-85937-523-5	£14.99	Glastonbury (pb)	1-85937-338-0	£7.99
Canals And Waterways (pb)	1-85937-291-0	£9.99	Gloucester (pb)	1-85937-232-5	£9.99
Canterbury Cathedral (pb)	1-85937-179-5	£9.99	Gloucestershire (pb)	1-85937-561-8	£9.99
Cardiff (pb)	1-85937-093-4	£9.99	Great Yarmouth (pb)	1-85937-426-3	£9.99
Carmarthenshire (pb)	1-85937-604-5	£9.99	Greater Manchester (pb)	1-85937-266-x	£9.99
Chelmsford (pb)	1-85937-310-0	£9.99	Guildford (pb)	1-85937-410-7	£9.99
Cheltenham (pb)	1-85937-095-0	£9.99	Hampshire (pb)	1-85937-279-1	£9.99
Cheshire (pb)	1-85937-271-6	£9.99	Harrogate (pb)	1-85937-423-9	£9.99
Chester (pb)	1-85937-382 8	£9.99	Hastings and Bexhill (pb)	1-85937-131-0	£9.99
Chesterfield (pb)	1-85937-378-x	£9.99	Heart of Lancashire (pb)	1-85937-197-3	£9.99
Chichester (pb)	1-85937-228-7	£9.99	Helston (pb)	1-85937-214-7	£9.99
Churches of East Cornwall (pb)	1-85937-249-x	£9.99	Hereford (pb)	1-85937-175-2	£9.99
Churches of Hampshire (pb)	1-85937-207-4	£9.99	Herefordshire (pb)	1-85937-567-7	£9.99
Cinque Ports & Two Ancient Towns	1-85937-492-1	£14.99	Herefordshire Living Memories	1-85937-514-6	£14.99
Colchester (pb)	1-85937-188-4	£8.99	Hertfordshire (pb)	1-85937-247-3	£9.99
Cornwall (pb)	1-85937-229-5	£9.99	Horsham (pb)	1-85937-432-8	£9.99
Cornwall Living Memories	1-85937-248-1	£14.99	Humberside (pb)	1-85937-605-3	£9.99
Cotswolds (pb)	1-85937-230-9	£9.99	Hythe, Romney Marsh, Ashford (pb)	1-85937-256-2	£9.99
Cotswolds Living Memories	1-85937-255-4	£14.99	Ipswich (pb)	1-85937-424-7	£9.99
County Durham (pb)	1-85937-398-4	£9.99	Isle of Man (pb)	1-85937-268-6	£9.99
Croydon Living Memories (pb)	1-85937-162-0	£9.99	Isle of Wight (pb)	1-85937-429-8	£9.99
Cumbria (pb)	1-85937-621-5	£9.99	Isle of Wight Living Memories	1-85937-304-6	£14.99
Derby (pb)	1-85937-367-4	£9.99	Kent (pb)	1-85937-189-2	£9.99
Derbyshire (pb)	1-85937-196-5	£9.99	Kent Living Memories(pb)	1-85937-401-8	£9.99
Derbyshire Living Memories	1-85937-330-5	£14.99	Kings Lynn (pb)	1-85937-334-8	£9.99

Available from your local bookshop or from the publisher

Title	ISBN	Price	Title	ISBN	Price
Lake District (pb)	1-85937-275-9	£9.99	Sherborne (pb)	1-85937-301-1	£9.99
Lancashire Living Memories	1-85937-335-6	£14.99	Shrewsbury (pb)	1-85937-325-9	£9.99
Lancaster, Morecambe, Heysham (pb)	1-85937-233-3	£9.99	Shropshire (pb)	1-85937-326-7	£9.99
Leeds (pb)	1-85937-202-3	£9.99	Shropshire Living Memories	1-85937-643-6	£14.99
Leicester (pb)	1-85937-381-x	£9.99	Somerset	1-85937-153-1	£14.99
Leicestershire & Rutland Living Memories	1-85937-500-6	£12.99	South Devon Coast	1-85937-107-8	£14.99
Leicestershire (pb)	1-85937-185-x	£9.99	South Devon Living Memories (pb)	1-85937-609-6	£9.99
Lighthouses	1-85937-257-0	£9.99	South East London (pb)	1-85937-263-5	£9.99
Lincoln (pb)	1-85937-380-1	£9.99	South Somerset	1-85937-318-6	£14.99
Lincolnshire (pb)	1-85937-433-6	£9.99	South Wales	1-85937-519-7	£14.99
Liverpool and Merseyside (pb)	1-85937-234-1	£9.99	Southampton (pb)	1-85937-427-1	£9.99
London (pb)	1-85937-183-3	£9.99	Southend (pb)	1-85937-313-5	£9.99
London Living Memories	1-85937-454-9	£14.99	Southport (pb)	1-85937-425-5	£9.99
Ludlow (pb)	1-85937-176-0	£9.99	St Albans (pb)	1-85937-341-0	£9.99
Luton (pb)	1-85937-235-x	£9.99	St Ives (pb)	1-85937-415-8	£9.99
Maidenhead (pb)	1-85937-339-9	£9.99	Stafford Living Memories (pb)	1-85937-503-0	£9.99
Maidstone (pb)	1-85937-391-7	£9.99	Staffordshire (pb)	1-85937-308-9	£9.99
Manchester (pb)	1-85937-198-1	£9.99	Stourbridge (pb)	1-85937-530-8	£9.99
Marlborough (pb)	1-85937-336-4	£9.99	Stratford upon Avon (pb)	1-85937-388-7	£9.99
Middlesex	1-85937-158-2	£14.99	Suffolk (pb)	1-85937-221-x	£9.99
Monmouthshire	1-85937-532-4	£14.99	Suffolk Coast (pb)	1-85937-610-x	£9.99
New Forest (pb)	1-85937-390-9	£9.99	Surrey (pb)	1-85937-240-6	£9.99
Newark (pb)	1-85937-366-6	£9.99	Surrey Living Memories	1-85937-328-3	£14.99
Newport, Wales (pb)	1-85937-258-9	£9.99	Sussex (pb)	1-85937-184-1	£9.99
Newquay (pb)	1-85937-421-2	£9.99	Sutton (pb)	1-85937-337-2	£9.99
Norfolk (pb)	1-85937-195-7	£9.99	Swansea (pb)	1-85937-167-1	£9.99
Norfolk Broads	1-85937-486-7	£14.99	Taunton (pb)	1-85937-314-3	£9.99
Norfolk Living Memories (pb)	1-85937-402-6	£9.99	Tees Valley & Cleveland (pb)	1-85937-623-1	£9.99
North Buckinghamshire	1-85937-626-6	£14.99	Teignmouth (pb)	1-85937-370-4	£7.99
North Devon Living Memories	1-85937-261-9	£14.99	Thanet (pb)	1-85937-116-7	£9.99
North Hertfordshire	1-85937-547-2	£14.99	Tiverton (pb)	1-85937-178-7	£9.99
North London (pb)	1-85937-403-4	£9.99	Torbay (pb)	1-85937-597-9	£9.99
North Somerset	1-85937-302-x	£14.99	Truro (pb)	1-85937-598-7	£9.99
North Wales (pb)	1-85937-298-8	£9.99	Victorian & Edwardian Dorset	1-85937-254-6	£14.99
North Yorkshire (pb)	1-85937-236-8	£9.99	Victorian & Edwardian Kent (pb)	1-85937-624-X	£9.99
Northamptonshire Living Memories	1-85937-529-4	£14.99	Victorian & Edwardian Maritime Album (pb)	1-85937-622-3	£9.99
Northamptonshire	1-85937-150-7	£14.99	Victorian and Edwardian Sussex (pb)	1-85937-625-8	£9.99
Northumberland Tyne & Wear (pb)	1-85937-281-3	£9.99	Villages of Devon (pb)	1-85937-293-7	£9.99
Northumberland	1-85937-522-7	£14.99	Villages of Kent (pb)	1-85937-294-5	£9.99
Norwich (pb)	1-85937-194-9	£8.99	Villages of Sussex (pb)	1-85937-295-3	£9.99
Nottingham (pb)	1-85937-324-0	£9.99	Warrington (pb)	1-85937-507-3	£9.99
Nottinghamshire (pb)	1-85937-187-6	£9.99	Warwick (pb)	1-85937-518-9	£9.99
Oxford (pb)	1-85937-411-5	£9.99	Warwickshire (pb)	1-85937-203-1	£9.99
Oxfordshire (pb)	1-85937-430-1	£9.99	Welsh Castles (pb)	1-85937-322-4	£9.99
Oxfordshire Living Memories	1-85937-525-1	£14.99	West Midlands (pb)	1-85937-289-9	£9.99
Paignton (pb)	1-85937-374-7	£7.99	West Sussex (pb)	1-85937-607-x	£9.99
Peak District (pb)	1-85937-280-5	£9.99	West Yorkshire (pb)	1-85937-201-5	£9.99
Pembrokeshire	1-85937-262-7	£14.99	Weston Super Mare (pb)	1-85937-306-2	£9.99
Penzance (pb)	1-85937-595-2	£9.99	Weymouth (pb)	1-85937-209-0	£9.99
Peterborough (pb)	1-85937-219-8	£9.99	Wiltshire (pb)	1-85937-277-5	£9.99
Picturesque Harbours	1-85937-208-2	£14.99	Wiltshire Churches (pb)	1-85937-171-x	£9.99
Piers	1-85937-237-6	£17.99	Wiltshire Living Memories (pb)	1-85937-396-8	£9.99
Plymouth (pb)	1-85937-389-5	£9.99	Winchester (pb)	1-85937-428-x	£9.99
Preston (pb)	1-85937-212-0	£9.99	Wokingham & Bracknell (pb)	1-85937-329-1	£9.99
Redhill to Reigate (pb)	1-85937-596-0	£9.99	Worcester (pb)	1-85937-165-5	£9.99
Ringwood (pb)	1-85937-384-4	£7.99	Worcestershire Living Memories	1-85937-489-1	£14.99
Romford (pb)	1-85937-319-4	£9.99	Worcestershire	1-85937-152-3	£14.99
Royal Tunbridge Wells (pb)	1-85937-504-9	£9.99	York (pb)	1-85937-199-x	£9.99
Salisbury (pb)	1-85937-239-2	£9.99	Yorkshire (pb)	1-85937-186-8	£9.99
Scarborough (pb)	1-85937-379-8	£9.99	Yorkshire Coastal Memories	1-85937-506-5	£14.99
Sevenoaks and Tonbridge (pb)	1-85937-392-5	£9.99	Yorkshire Dales	1-85937-502-2	£14.99
Sheffield & South Yorks (pb)	1-85937-267-8	£9.99	Yorkshire Living Memories (pb)	1-85937-397-6	£9.99

See Frith books on the internet at www.francisfrith.co.uk

FRITH PRODUCTS & SERVICES

Francis Frith would doubtless be pleased to know that the pioneering publishing venture he started in 1860 still continues today. Over a hundred and forty years later, The Francis Frith Collection continues in the same innovative tradition and is now one of the foremost publishers of vintage photographs in the world. Some of the current activities include:

Interior Decoration

Today Frith's photographs can be seen framed and as giant wall murals in thousands of pubs, restaurants, hotels, banks, retail stores and other public buildings throughout the country. In every case they enhance the unique local atmosphere of the places they depict and provide reminders of gentler days in an increasingly busy and frenetic world.

Product Promotions

Frith products are used by many major companies to promote the sales of their own products or to reinforce their own history and heritage. Frith promotions have been used by Hovis bread, Courage beers, Scots Porage Oats, Colman's mustard, Cadbury's foods, Mellow Birds coffee, Dunhill pipe tobacco, Guinness, and Bulmer's Cider.

Genealogy and Family History

As the interest in family history and roots grows world-wide, more and more people are turning to Frith's photographs of Great Britain for images of the towns, villages and streets where their ancestors lived; and, of course, photographs of the churches and chapels where their ancestors were christened, married and buried are an essential part of every genealogy tree and family album.

Frith Products

All Frith photographs are available Framed or just as Mounted Prints and Posters (size 23 x 16 inches). These may be ordered from the address below. From time to time other products - Address Books, Calendars, Table Mats, etc - are available.

The Internet

Already fifty thousand Frith photographs can be viewed and purchased on the internet through the Frith websites and a myriad of partner sites.

For more detailed information on Frith companies and products, look at these sites:

www.francisfrith.co.uk
www.francisfrith.com
(for North American visitors)

See the complete list of Frith Books at:

www.francisfrith.co.uk

This web site is regularly updated with the latest list of publications from the Frith Book Company. If you wish to buy books relating to another part of the country that your local bookshop does not stock, you may purchase on-line.

For further information, trade, or author enquiries please contact us at the address below:
The Francis Frith Collection, Frith's Barn, Teffont, Salisbury, Wiltshire, England SP3 5QP.
Tel: +44 (0)1722 716 376 Fax: +44 (0)1722 716 881 Email: sales@francisfrith.co.uk

See Frith books on the internet at www.francisfrith.co.uk